The New Rules of Dining Out

AN INSIDER'S
GUIDE TO
ENJOYING
RESTAURANTS

The New Rules of Dining Out

ADAM REINER

LOUISIANA STATE UNIVERSITY PRESS   BATON ROUGE

Published with the assistance of The Noland Fund

Published by Louisiana State University Press
lsupress.org

Manufactured in the United States of America
First printing

Designer: Barbara Neely Bourgoyne
Typefaces: Dolly Pro, text; Take Me to Tuscany and Metropolis, display
Printer and binder: Sheridan Books

Cover illustration: AdobeStock/GarkushaArt.

Cataloging-in-Publication Data are available from the Library of Congress.
ISBN 978-0-8071-8504-9 (cloth: alk. paper) — ISBN 978-0-8071-8560-5 (pdf) —
ISBN 978-0-8071-8559-9 (epub)

For L.G.

Menu

PREFACE

When Emily Post's book *Etiquette: In Society, in Business, in Politics, and at Home* was published in July 1922, it spurred a national conversation about manners. Post had already published several novels to little acclaim; nothing she'd ever written came even close to *Etiquette*'s success. The book, which sold over one and a half million copies during her lifetime, demonstrated that Americans were not only open to the idea that there was inherent value in practicing proper etiquette but were also willing to accept that refining one's social graces could help foster more fruitful social interactions, better first impressions, and healthier interpersonal relationships.

Among other kernels of wisdom, the book's first edition contains advice on how to sit gracefully ("one should not perch stiffly on the edge of a straight chair, nor sprawl at length in an easy one") and the importance of keeping a dinner engagement ("nothing but serious illness or death or an utterly unavoidable accident can excuse the breaking of a dinner engagement"). Post dedicates entire chapters to the finer points of hosting dinner parties, proper table settings, and etiquette for weddings, funerals, and golf outings. As an arbiter of good manners, she single-handedly helped canonize common courtesies such as keeping one's elbows off the dinner table or chewing with one's mouth closed. I was surprised to find that early editions of *Etiquette* hardly mention restaurants.

Last year, my curiosity brought me to the Rare Book Division of the New York Public Library, where I requisitioned a 1924 print edition of *Etiquette* to see if Post had any advice about refining restaurant manners.

Despite the volume's six hundred–plus frayed and yellowing pages, I could only find eight entries for the word *restaurant* in the index. Most of those entries related to proper dress code. "Restaurant dress depends on the restaurant and the city," Post writes on page 556. "Because women in New York wear low-necked dresses and no hats, does not mean that those who live in New Town should do the same, if it is not New Town's custom." (I do not know whether New Town is an actual town or if Post refers to it generically.) On page 569, she includes tuxedos among a list of garments that she considers proper restaurant attire for men, a testament to the fact that fine dining in the 1920s was still an unfamiliar extravagance to most average Americans.

What impresses me most about Post's work more than a hundred years after she published it is the populist message lingering beneath her ideology, which on the surface might be easily dismissible as elitist. "A knowledge of etiquette is of course essential to one's decent behavior, just as clothing is essential to one's decent appearance," Post writes, "and precisely as one wears the latter without being self-conscious of having on shoes and perhaps gloves, one who has good manners is equally unself-conscious in the observance of etiquette, the precepts of which must be so thoroughly absorbed as to make their observance a matter of instinct rather than of conscious obedience."

While the idea of reading a book about etiquette may seem antiquated today, in my mind, there's no reason we shouldn't have the same curiosity about how our behavior in restaurants affects the quality of our dining experiences. As someone who's worked in restaurants for more than two decades, I've seen firsthand how engaging more mindfully can improve the quality of one's service, from fostering deeper connections with staff to more effectively communicating one's needs. Dining in a restaurant, more so than other service-oriented transactions, brings with it a unique level of intimacy that makes our behavior even more integral to the success or failure of these experiences.

Restaurants have become much more centered in modern culture than they were during Emily Post's lifetime. In 2022, her great-great-grandchildren Lizzie Post and Daniel Post Senning celebrated the book's centennial anniversary by releasing a revised edition of *Etiquette* with advice on modern-day manners such as how to address people using proper pronouns and how to unfriend personal connections on social media. Unlike the original volume, the modern edition acknowledges the importance of restaurants in contemporary life with more nuanced discussion around how customers should behave when they dine out.

In a section entitled "Out to Eat," Post's heirs acknowledge that today's broader spectrum of restaurant experiences—from fine dining to fast casual—can make understanding the rules of engagement quite difficult. "Feeling confident navigating the type of dining-out experience will allow you to relax and enjoy your time with others," they write. "When you're confident in your social skills in a given situation, the focus can be on the good time you're all having." But aside from commentary on topics such as dividing the bill, tipping properly, and what to do when you make a mess, the book hardly scratches the surface on how readers can become better restaurant guests.

Even though neither the original nor the updated edition of *Etiquette* offer much commentary on how to behave in restaurants, what Post did a century ago, quite admirably so, was to provide a framework for readers to acquire and practice better manners. My hope is that restaurant enthusiasts like you will approach this book with the same curiosity and open-mindedness that Post's readers did in 1922.

Like *Etiquette*, this book travels relatively uncharted waters. There have been quite a few short-form articles written about restaurant etiquette in publications such as *Food & Wine* magazine and *Bon Appétit*, but no one has endeavored to compile all that knowledge into a "Diner's Bible." There are plenty of books dedicated to the art of hospitality, like Danny Meyer's *Setting the Table*, but considering how popular dining out has become, it comes as a surprise that no one has ever dedicated an entire book to how we can get better at it.

By examining certain restaurant scenarios from an insider's perspective, this book will encourage you to think differently about what makes your restaurant experiences successful. More than anything, it should help you understand why being an active participant in your dining experiences, a more engaged and compassionate guest, will result in more fruitful restaurant visits. When you finish reading this book, you should have a new perspective about what makes an exemplary restaurant customer.

In the restaurant industry, we often refer to our customers as guests. We do this because it's important to make everyone feel like a guest in our home. But unfortunately, our guests don't always display the same humility as they would as guests in a friend's home. No matter how much effort a restaurant staff puts into delivering a seamless dining experience, the true magic of dining out cannot be unleashed without you, the guest, actively participating. There is always one constant variable in every single one of your restaurant experiences: *you*. This makes your attitude and your behavior among the two most important factors in whether your dining experience is successful or not.

When we want to become better cooks, we buy cookbooks and seek guidance from chefs. But there is no equivalent to a cookbook for how we can become better diners. That's because most of us don't think of dining out as a skill we can improve. But I believe we can. Much the same way that Emily Post provided her readers a framework that helped them cultivate better manners, this book offers parameters that will help you dine with greater dexterity. Reading this book should benefit you the same way that *Etiquette* did for curious readers in 1922, by helping you better understand the rules of engagement in a restaurant setting.

You will not agree with everything you read in these pages, but my hope is that the book will encourage positive habits that will lead you to have more productive restaurant experiences. Among other lessons in the coming chapters, you'll learn how to become a more mindful guest, engage more gracefully with staff, better communicate your needs, ask the right questions, tip more effectively, and avoid pitfalls that can sabotage a great meal. The good news is that aside from asking you to keep an open mind, these lessons won't require any serious effort on your part, other than embracing the possibility that you can improve yourself as a restaurant guest. I promise you it's worth it.

The New Rules of Dining Out

Introduction

As a restaurateur, my job is to basically
control the chaos and the drama. There's always going
to be chaos in the restaurant business.

—ROCCO DISPIRITO

It's a few minutes past 8:00 p.m. A crowd of ravenous and impatient guests are packed like sardines in the tiny bar area. Some of them have been waiting for over an hour to be seated. I force my way through the mass of bodies, balancing a tray of martinis as I angle toward the cavernous back room of the restaurant. It's been at least twenty minutes since table 30 finished their appetizers, and their next course still hasn't arrived. My pulse quickens, and the collar of my starchy tuxedo shirt dampens with sweat. I'm afraid to go back into the kitchen to check on my food. Twenty minutes might not seem like a long time to wait for food in a restaurant, but restaurant time is different from real time. When someone's food is dragging, minutes seem like hours. In my twenty-year career waiting tables, I've learned that nothing destroys a perfectly enjoyable dining experience quicker than a table's food taking too long. Every restaurant worker has horror stories about customers melting down over service delays. In these moments, it feels like all the oxygen is being sucked out of the room. With every passing moment that a table waits, their hunger turns to anger, and their patience turns to despair.

I'm a captain at one of the most popular restaurants in New York City, an absurdly overpriced red sauce joint in the West Village. We're called captains—a fancified word that applies to some fine dining waiters—but this isn't your run-of-the-mill server job. On any given night, members of the Kardashian or Jenner family might drop in unannounced. Drake even rapped about the restaurant in one of his songs. Everything on the menu is grotesquely expensive, but you're paying for the privilege, not the veal parmesan. As a captain, my job is to make people feel at ease about how much money they're spending. If I do my job well, they'll leave spending much more than they wanted to, and they won't feel cheated.

My anxiety about the delay with table 30's food is exacerbated by the fact that they're waiting for a course of fresh pasta with shaved white truffles, which, at $175 per order, is the most expensive item on the menu. When I sold them on the truffle idea earlier, I promised to have the kitchen split three orders of the pasta into half-portions so that all six people at the table could have an individual plate. It seemed like a small sacrifice in exchange for them spending over $500 on a single course of food. The family is celebrating the youngest's high school graduation, and the graduate's proud father—who's made it known several times that the bill should come to him—is very adamant about her special night going perfectly, without a hitch.

For the uninitiated, white truffles are a seasonal delicacy, a mushroomlike fungus in the tuber family that can only be harvested underground in a few isolated places on earth, most famously in the woodlands of Northern Italy. Truffles can't be cultivated. In fact, they are so hard to find that they require trained truffle-sniffing dogs to unearth them, a rarity that in certain seasons can cost up to three thousand dollars a pound. Chefs prefer to serve truffles unadorned, over simple dishes like fresh pasta in butter sauce, soft scrambled eggs, and creamy polenta. Affluent diners are willing to spend exorbitant sums for the privilege of indulging in white truffles during their fleeting season from late fall into early winter and regard them with the same reverence as other luxury items such as caviar and Wagyu beef.

The restaurant where I work is a destination, almost every table is celebrating a special occasion—a birthday, anniversary, wedding, quinceañera, promotion, or other major life event. The pressure to exceed expectations is constant. But when parties like table 30 are in a celebratory mood, they also reward you by opening their wallets more widely and tipping profusely. Before I started waiting tables in high-end restaurants, I had no idea that anyone spent thousands of dollars on a single restaurant meal. But at places like this one, it happens every night. Still, it's a strange feeling to drop checks when guests are spending more on dinner than the average person's monthly rent.

I gaze toward the kitchen entrance like an aggravated straphanger staring blankly into the hollow void of a dark subway tunnel with no trains in sight. As a server, when your table's food is taking too long, there is nowhere to hide. I've witnessed panicked waiters lock themselves in the bathroom simply to avoid an impatient table's scorn. I resist the urge to check my watch. The actual time is meaningless. How long table 30's been waiting for their food doesn't matter. If they call me over to the table and say, "Excuse me, we've been waiting for over a half an hour for our next course!" I could not respond, "I'm sorry, but you're exaggerating—it's only been *fifteen* minutes." In restaurants, the guest's perception is always our reality.

At the end of the day, the primary function of a restaurant is to feed people. If it fails at that basic purpose, then nothing else matters. Before table 30's pasta course went mysteriously missing, they adored me. I talked them through the menu and expertly answered all their questions. I recommended dishes tailored to their specific food preferences and dietary restrictions. They even complimented my tuxedo, which I demurely agreed looks very handsome on me.

Now I'm afraid to make eye contact. They're starting to look around, and I can feel the anger bubbling like an overheated pot of marinara sauce. I gave them the hard sell on the truffle pasta, and now that it's missing, I've become the fall guy. I sidle over to the table to gently reassure them that the pasta should be arriving any moment. Waiters make a living by saying what people want to hear. The good ones are smart enough not to dig their own graves.

After another ten minutes pass, the father beckons me to the table and asks, with a wry smirk, if the chef needed to fly to Italy to unearth the white truffles himself. I force a smile, even though I've heard similar jokes countless times before. When food is taking too long, disenchanted guests often ask cheeky rhetorical questions—"Is the chef catching my fish in the Hudson River?" or "Are they hunting for my duck in Central Park?" Sarcastic remarks like these usually signify a restaurant meltdown in its embryonic stages. The meltdowns go nuclear when people are spending a lot of money. Table 30's check is already well over $1,000. They've ordered two bottles of Brunello di Montalcino, a Tuscan red that costs $250 per bottle.

"What's going on with table 30?" my manager snaps at me. "Have you checked with Chef about their truffle pasta?" He has to ask, but he knows I haven't checked with Chef because Chef doesn't take kindly to frivolous interruptions about food delays. For waiters who value their sanity, entering the kitchen when your table's food is taking too long is always a last resort. But my manager asks me anyway because his job is to put out fires before they happen, and feigning concern helps justify his otherwise meaningless existence. There is no more thankless job in the world than restaurant manager. You're basically a glorified babysitter for a staff of spoiled waiters who make twice as much money as you and work half as many hours.

Servers in most fine dining restaurants generally try to avoid direct contact with the chef during service. Not all chefs are temperamental, of course. But a professional kitchen is a highly stressful environment, and some chefs handle the pressure better than others. No chef can afford unnecessary distractions. It's why many chefs are easily annoyed when anyone not wearing chef whites enters their kitchen to make a frivolous request ("Chef, is it possible to take the skin off the whole grilled branzino for table 45? This woman is grossed out by fish skin") or to lament over the whereabouts of their table's food. "Everything's working!" the irritated chef will say, which means: "I appreciate your concern. Now kindly *get the hell out of my kitchen!*" Through sheer force of habit, I choose not to bother the chef about table 30's truffle pasta, which turns out to be a very inauspicious decision.

When my manager finally checks with the kitchen on my behalf, he learns that the expediter, whose role it is to orchestrate the orderly firing of tables (in kitchen parlance, *firing* refers to the verbal instructions the expediter gives to the line cooks to begin preparing a table's food), accidently spiked the fire ticket for their pasta course. That explains why table 30's pasta is nowhere to be found. When the expediter "spikes" a fire ticket, it signifies that a table's food has left the kitchen. Since the expediter inadvertently spiked the fire ticket for table 30's pasta course, the kitchen assumed that the food had already gone out. (In this case, the fire ticket is a small paper chit that reads **FIRE Table 30** which gets spiked over an upright metal prod next to the pass when the food goes out.) At this point, laying blame is pointless. All that matters is that hundreds of dollars' worth of white truffle pasta are missing, and my table is about to have a conniption.

Whenever mistakes like this are made in a restaurant, the staff hopes that showering the table with free food and drink will help ameliorate the situation. The pasta station is slammed with other orders, so it'll be at least another ten minutes before the pasta hits the table. Chef sends out a complimentary roasted beet salad with pistachios to table 30 as an olive branch. They don't like beets. Of course they don't. No one likes beets. The beet salad is by far the worst-selling dish on the menu, which is why the chef is giving it away. He needs to get rid of it. No one at table 30 even touches the plate.

As the wait grows longer, the father gets up from the table and corners me in the wait station. "What is happening with our food? This is outrageous." I take a deep breath. "Sir, I'm very sorry for the delay—" But before I can finish my apology, he interrupts: "If the pasta doesn't arrive in five minutes, we're leaving!" I notice a swollen blue vein protruding below the crest of his receding hairline in the shape of a thunderbolt. "My manager has assured me that your pastas will be arriving any moment," I say solemnly. "I really appreciate your patience." By mentioning my manager, I hope it will deflect some of the pressure away from me. I can see his jaw tightening. "Why is it so difficult to cook a simple pasta?" he asks in a hushed, menacing tone. If I thought it would do any good, I'd explain that asking *why* in a restaurant is a pointless exercise. Sometimes there isn't a why. Restaurants aren't rational.

But I also understand that waiters are paid to have answers. Unfortunately, the real explanation is too technical and wouldn't make the pasta materialize any faster. I can't say, "Sir, unfortunately, someone in the kitchen spiked the fire ticket." *Fire ticket? What the heck is a fire ticket?* Before returning to the table, the father stops at the podium and asks the maître d' to send a manager over to the table. When a guest asks to speak with a manager, the battle has been lost. As they say when contestants are eliminated from *Top Chef*, "Please pack your knives and go." I overhear the man telling my manager that I've "ruined his daughter's graduation party." He reiterates his threat to leave if the pasta isn't served immediately. My manager does his best to deescalate the situation, assuring the man that the entire pasta course—several hundred dollars' worth of food—will be comped. He promises to send the sommelier with a fresh bottle of wine for the table, also complimentary. As the conversation becomes more animated, guests seated at the surrounding tables are distracted by the commotion, shifting around in their seats and looking relieved that their food is on the table.

Moments later, the pasta finally arrives. The food runners deliver the plates in perfect synchrony, and my manager generously shaves a white truffle the size of a racquetball over each pasta dish. Normally, the spectacle of truffle shavings raining down would be met with a chorus of oohs and aahs, but the vibe at the table is about as cheerful as a funeral reception. They eat the rest of their meal in somber silence. I do my best to keep the mood cheerful, but it feels like being on a first date with someone who isn't attracted to you. As expected, they refuse dessert. "I don't think we have another hour to kill for a slice of cheesecake," one of the guests mutters under his breath.

We send a complimentary chocolate layer cake with a candle on a plate that has "Congratulations!" written in chocolate script for the guest of honor. But no one is in a mood to celebrate anymore, including me. They abruptly ask for the check without finishing the cake, which I present with almost eight hundred dollars' worth of comped food and wine. I don't even need to look at the signed credit card receipt to know they haven't left a tip.

Let me be clear: table 30 was not wrong for being upset. Forty minutes is a shamefully long time to wait for a pasta course. The restaurant undeniably failed to provide these guests with a seamless experience, and admittedly, I'd been negligent by not checking on their food sooner.

But it's still possible for a table in a situation like theirs to enjoy themselves even when the restaurant executes as poorly as we did or when the quality of the food or service doesn't meet their expectations. Everyone's threshold for tolerating mistakes is different. Some diners are more charitable than others when mistakes are made, and some mistakes are harder to forgive.

But the biggest mistake that guests often make is assuming that when a restaurant experience disappoints, as exemplified by the scenario I've just described, the root of the problem is incompetence. The truth is, most of the time when mistakes happen in restaurants, they are honest and accidental. In this case, aside from not being proactive enough about communicating with the kitchen about my table's missing food, I wasn't directly responsible for what went wrong. I sent the fire ticket to the kitchen on time, and it never should have been spiked without the food leaving the kitchen.

Ultimately, table 30's "ruined" meal is just one in a million restaurant experiences that didn't end up going exactly as planned. Restaurants are designed to function like well-oiled machines, and sometimes those machines unexpectedly break down. But this party's experience didn't have to devolve into something irreconcilable. I think if more diners understood what was going on behind the scenes in these situations, they would respond more charitably to hiccups in service and be more empathetic when mistakes happen. The more I experienced these kinds of mishaps while working in restaurants, the more I thought about the guest's role in reclaiming a negative experience. No matter how much the staff tries to rescue a crisis like this one, if a guest chooses to be miserable, there is simply nothing we can do.

Restaurants are fragile ecosystems. Minor disturbances with one table's meal have a way of disturbing the peace at other tables. Everything is interconnected. But the natural state of a restaurant is chaos. The staff basically exists to shield guests from the chaos the best they can. There is an inherent thrill behind relinquishing control and entrusting strangers to cook and serve for you, but it also requires a great deal of trust and an understanding that things can and will go wrong. Society's deeply ingrained ideas about hospitality have conditioned guests to believe that restaurants bear full responsibility for the success or failure of their meal.

As someone who has spent over two decades working in some of the country's finest restaurants, I've observed all kinds of customer behavior, from a girlfriend dousing her partner in red wine after a lover's quarrel to a grown man throwing a temper tantrum over the restaurant's choice to play Led Zeppelin music on the stereo. These experiences have taught me that how guests engage with staff can impact the outcome of their dining experience. I don't mean exchanging pleasantries, like profusely thanking every busser who clears a dirty plate or politely asking a staff member for directions to the restroom. I'm referring to the energy and attitude that every guest brings to the table when they dine out and how their behavior either positively or negatively affects the quality of their service.

My time in restaurants has also taught me that most diners don't give very much thought to how they engage with staff. Too often, guests expect servers to be unconditionally accommodating and to exhibit limitless grace. Even a seemingly harmless gesture, such as ignoring a server's greeting to ask for the Wi-Fi password, may be misconstrued as standoffishness. Any signs of ambivalence can mislead servers into falsely assuming that you don't value their input or that you'd prefer to be left alone. I've found that these first impressions are easily squandered. But they should be viewed as opportunities.

As a waiter, I have often found myself wishing that I could pull misguided guests aside for some one-on-one coaching to show them how they could've better conveyed a special request or registered a complaint more effectively. If someone's habit is to immediately ask for water without ice without as much as a hello, I might suggest that they wait until *after* they order drinks or discuss the menu with the server to make such requests. Developing a rapport with the server and aligning your priorities is much more important than making demands about your water preferences.

It's hard for some people to give up control when they dine out. That tension becomes especially pronounced when things go awry. But how you handle yourself in the face of unexpected turbulence can affect how smooth the landing is. The difference between saying "Excuse me, we've been waiting forever for our appetizers!" or asking "Would you mind checking on our appetizers? It feels like it's been a while" is more significant than most diners think. When your food is over-seasoned, summoning the server to say, "This dish is so salty—all I can taste is salt!" is not as productive, or graceful, as saying, "This dish is seasoned a bit too heavily for my taste—could I look at the menu again? I think I'd like to order something else." I'm sad to report that in my experience, too many guests employ the more hyperbolic approach.

You're not alone if you think that the staff's job is to do whatever is necessary to make guests happy, but the old adage "The customer is always right" hasn't aged gracefully. We all have family members who rage at customer service representatives when they feel shortchanged because they're conditioned to think that raising their voice is the most effective way to get results. Being abusive might prompt management to send over a free round of drinks or a dessert on the house as a pacifier, but any reparations often come at the expense of the customer's reputation. That can matter the next time this person requests a reservation. Abusive guests are rarely forgotten. As dining out becomes a more serious pursuit, many diners have become harder to please, which can put undue strain on staff, who are often expected to satisfy guests who come in with unrealistic expectations.

During the 1990s, restaurants began to take on a deeper cultural significance in America. Televised cooking shows such as *Essence of Emeril* and *The Naked Chef*, which proliferated with the launch of the Food Network in 1993, supercharged the public's interest in gourmet food and international cuisine. Of course, precursors to those shows, Graham Kerr's *The Galloping Gourmet* and Julia Child's *The French Chef*, paved the way for the culinary revolution. But decades later, a new crop of charismatic young food personalities like Guy Fieri and Rachel Ray democratized it. Still, for the greater part of the twentieth century, chefs were a lowly caste; the job was widely considered an undesirable vocation reserved for transients and outcasts.

I'm reminded of an (unpublished) interview I once had with the legendary chef Jacques Pépin in which we discussed his mentor, friend, and colleague the late chef Pierre Franey. Pépin stressed that the concept of a celebrity chef is not nearly as contemporary as most food enthusiasts would like to believe. "I was the personal chef for three heads of state in France between 1956 and 1958, including Charles de Gaulle—not once did I ever have an interview with a magazine or newspaper," Pépin told me. "That did not exist. A cook was in the back of the kitchen, period. No one would ever call the chef for kudos in the dining room. If anyone came into the kitchen, it was to complain because something went wrong."

If not for Anthony Bourdain and his gifts for finding poetry in the grit of professional kitchens and the motley crew of outsiders who worked in them, restaurant chefs might have remained relegated to society's fringes. Bourdain, an adroit observer and cultural interlocutor, offered readers an uncensored and intimate view of restaurant life from an insider's perspective. In doing so, he also helped fuel the public's growing obsession with restaurants and chefs.

The digital age has had an immeasurable effect on our comportment in the dining room. The atmosphere of a bustling restaurant was already a spectacle, but smartphones (and perhaps soon, wearable technology like augmented reality glasses) have turned restaurants into backdrops for social media content. Many diners take more photographs with their food than they do with their friends. We used to go out for dinner and a show; now dinner *is* the show.

In response to these rapidly changing dining habits, I launched my blog, the *Restaurant Manifesto*, in 2014. My goal then was to shed light on the mysterious inner workings of a restaurant, hoping that sharing these insights might help people dine better. In addition to long-form essays about restaurant life and dining culture in America, I also wrote easily digestible dining tips—like never asking your server their name before introducing yourself—to help avid diners better manage their relationships with staff. The blog was embraced by restaurant industry types but gradually developed a following among everyday restaurant lovers too.

The New Rules of Dining Out is the product of my decades of experience working in restaurants and writing about them. Like many college graduates with uncertain career goals, I didn't choose the restaurant industry. It chose me. The flexible hours, consistent pay, and intoxicating flavors have an allure that I never could have experienced confined to a cubicle inside a dreary office all day. What kept me in the restaurant industry so long was the thrum of a busy dining room, the camaraderie among staff, and the opportunity to make a decent living without feeling trapped on a dead-end career path.

Restaurant work can be incredibly stressful but also extremely rewarding. Making people feel special is an exhilarating feeling that can be addictive. Once you've experienced the adrenaline rush of a busy Saturday night, working a normal nine-to-five job in more conventional industries can be difficult. A restaurant dining room is a cross section of humanity. Behind the scenes, you see it all—the good, the bad, and the ugly.

Try to approach this book with an open mind. In the coming pages, I'll question the established orthodoxy around hospitality put forth by industry leaders such as Danny Meyer and Will Guidara that, I think, de-emphasizes the role that guests play in the success or failure of their dining experiences. While it may be difficult to accept that customers should play a more active part in making these experiences special, I hope to convince you why it's always in your best interests to do so. I hope that sharing my insights about the inner workings of restaurants will help you understand certain scenarios from an insider's perspective and lead to some aha moments.

My other hope is that this book will stimulate a deeper conversation about how guests can learn to engage better in restaurants and become more mindful diners. The same things that make you a successful friend, lover, sibling, coworker, or spouse also make you a great restaurant guest. It starts with showing respect, patience, empathy, flexibility, and selflessness. But at the very minimum, it also requires *compliance*. If you exhibit these traits when you dine out, even when your food doesn't meet your expectations, you are much more likely to leave satisfied, even thrilled. Remember: you can have great experiences in bad restaurants, and you can have bad experiences in great restaurants.

This book is intended as a guide to help you avoid common pitfalls when you dine out while also helping foster healthy practices that will lead to better engagement with staff. Before we delve into ways you can improve as a diner, though, I think it's useful to reflect on the history of restaurants and the role they play in modern life as well as some over-arching principles that will help put you on the path toward becoming a better restaurant guest.

CHAPTER ONE

Restaurants Are More Important Than Ever

A restaurant is a fantasy—a kind of living fantasy in which
diners are the most important members of the cast.

—WARNER LEROY

Close your eyes and think about your favorite restaurant. For most of us, the mere thought triggers nostalgia and reverie. It makes us yearn for the sublime mushroom risotto made with fresh porcini we had in a trattoria outside of Chianti, swoon over the ethereal soup dumplings we had in Taipei that exploded like tiny broth grenades, pine for the buttery live lobsters we crack open freshly steamed off the docks every summer in Narraganset, or dream about the fluffy buttermilk pancakes slathered in wild blueberry syrup from the century-old diner in our hometown. Perhaps your fondest memories involve luxuriating in a generous booth table at Chili's or Applebee's, where your grandmother took you every Sunday after church, or devouring the dollar-menu McNuggets you drunkenly ordered in college at 2:00 a.m. when you were supposed to be writing a term paper. Restaurant food doesn't have to be fancy to be indelibly etched into our subconscious.

We love our favorite restaurants. We feel protective and possessive of them. We memorize their menus. We religiously order our favorite dishes every time—those sauerkraut pierogis that taste just like our *babunia* used to make or the tiramisu that takes us back to our honeymoon in Positano. When we visit these beloved places, the bartender remembers exactly how we like our martini. The soundtrack is always perfectly calibrated to our mood. Time slows down. Our cares float away.

When we return to our hometowns after long absences, revisiting our favorite restaurants—the tavern-style pizza joint, the kosher delicatessen, or the mom-and-pop soul food place—is always the first order of business. We're heartbroken when these beloved places close unexpectedly. When they do, it feels like we've lost a piece of our own personal history. We get emotionally attached to restaurants.

Despite the corrosive effects of the COVID-19 pandemic on the restaurant industry, Americans are dining out more than ever. In its most recent *State of the Restaurant Industry* report, the National Restaurant Association projects sales in the food service industry to reach record levels in 2025, topping $1.5 trillion for the first time in history. Whether they're dining in Michelin-starred, farm-to-table restaurants or fast casual concepts such as Sweetgreen and Shake Shack, Americans are eating outside of their homes in record numbers. For the most avid diners, discovering new restaurants has become a serious pastime. As such, dining expenses comprise a larger portion of Americans' discretionary income than they did several decades ago. According to a research report by World Metrics, Americans eat out in restaurants on average 4.3 times a week and spend over three thousand dollars on dining out each year. The study also found that 40 percent of respondents considered dining out their favorite way to spend free time.

As much as how we dress or how we style our hair, our restaurant choices reflect our own personal brands. The types of restaurants we prefer say a lot about who we are. Some experience nirvana in the drive-through of In-N-Out Burger; others feel most alive peering over the sushi counter of a hidden ten-seat omakase restaurant or driving fourteen hours through the Scandinavian wilderness to experience the taste of salt pork pancakes. Few activities are more interwoven into the fabric of how we socialize than dining out, and even fewer provoke the kind of primal catharsis that we regularly feel when restaurants delight us. More and more, our food choices have become integral to our identities.

While it may seem like restaurants have always been a fixture in American society, the modern restaurant is still a fairly new construct. According to historian and Yale professor Paul Freedman, in his book *Ten Restaurants That Changed America*, modern iterations of full-service, dine-in restaurants have only existed in the United States since the 1830s. Delmonico's in New York City, which began offering an à la carte menu in 1837, is widely considered the first contemporary restaurant in the United States. What made Delmonico's so unique, according to Freedman, was that it offered guests a menu with choices, a ubiquitous feature of modern dining that was unheard of at the time.

Freedman's book provides insights into how the modern concept of a restaurant, after emerging in France decades earlier, took shape in the United States beginning in the first half of the nineteenth century. "Unlike inns or boardinghouses which served meals at a single stated time," Freedman writes, "restaurants offered a range of times when patrons could show up and expect food." Delmonico's certainly didn't invent the concept of serving gourmet food in an elegant atmosphere. Fine French restaurants preceded it by almost a century. There were also much earlier examples of formal dining throughout Asia, dating back to the Song Dynasty in China, circa 1100 BCE. Today's intricately plated, elaborate tasting menus owe a debt to Japanese kaisekis, traditional multi-course meals that grew out of traditional Buddhist tea ceremonies during the sixteenth century.

But modern conveniences like private seating, individualized table service, and menu choice didn't become mainstream in the United States until the mid-nineteenth century. The earliest examples of restaurants, in fact, were comparatively quite primitive. Meals were served at standardized times, without customization, and seating was often communal. Delmonico's offered a new paradigm. "Rather than having to accept a set meal, the restaurant-goer could choose from a menu," Freedman writes, "and in place of the single communal table, customers ate with their own group in a public setting but set off from other parties." In the ensuing decades, the new format proliferated, especially in densely populated coastal cities such as New York and San Francisco. A new generation of American restaurants—including many that were owned and operated by immigrants like the Swiss-born Delmonico brothers—leaned heavily on European aesthetics in their cuisine, ambience, and hospitality.

What Is a Restaurant?

The word *restaurant* traces back to its humble beginnings as a restorative refuge. "The restaurant as a space of urban sociability emerged from the consommé," writes Rebecca Spang, the author of *The Invention of the Restaurant: Paris and Modern Gastronomic Culture.* "In the beginning, one went to a restaurant, or as they were commonly called, a 'restaurateur's room,' to drink restorative bouillons, as one went to a café to drink coffee." Very little food was sold in these primitive dining spaces, which were advertised as sanctuaries for the frail and infirmed. "In its initial form, then, a restaurant was specifically a place one went *not* to eat," Spang writes, "but to sit and weakly sip on one's *restaurant.*" In his book *In the Restaurant: Society in Four Courses,* Christoph Ribbat characterizes a modern restaurant as "a public space where people can eat when they want, what they want, and as much as they want for a previously established price." He offers the caveat, though, that restaurants must constantly adapt to shifting cultural trends, changing appetites, and economic realities. In recent decades, the definition of a restaurant has broadened as the industry adjusts to the changing needs of a food-obsessed, and often attention-deficient, population whose expectations of restaurants are higher than ever.

As restaurants become more centered in contemporary culture, modern diners approach restaurant visits as passionately as they do sporting events, fashion shows, and rock concerts. On the surface, dining out appears to be an activity that requires absolutely no skill—anyone with discretionary income and an appetite can participate. These days, epicureans traverse the globe in search of transformative dining experiences. A city's most sought-after restaurants have become must-see tourist destinations, on par with art museums and architectural landmarks. Gastronomy tourism, or gastro-tourism, has transformed the restaurant industry into a powerful engine of economic development and a leading indicator of the financial health of local economies.

In 2020, during the first six months of the COVID-19 pandemic, over 100,000 restaurants abruptly closed in the United States. Many of them never reopened. The mass extinction event provided a terrifying peek into a dystopian world without places to dine. Quarantined inside their homes for what seemed like an eternity, downtrodden gastronomes turned to sourdough starters and windowsill herb gardens to satisfy their culinary urges. But aside from the loss of precious lives during the pandemic, the absence of our favorite bars and restaurants turned out to be one of the most heartbreaking aspects of the lockdowns.

What the pandemic demonstrated in a dramatic way is how restaurants have become the nerve centers of our communities. They provide invaluable communal spaces for gathering with loved ones and collectively stand as living documents of our culinary and cultural history. Restaurants define the character of American cities—from the greasy spoon diner to the roadside BBQ pit to the family-owned taqueria to the Michelin-starred sushi counter. The convenience of enjoying prepared food—whether it comes from farm-to-table restaurants, street fairs, food trucks, vending machines, or gas stations—has become increasingly commoditized. In most major cities, we can summon couriers to deliver any world cuisine to our doorstep in minutes with a few simple taps on our smartphones.

The public has become more opinionated about restaurants too. We swear by our favorite places and pillory others. A new generation of "foodies" has emerged in recent years, raised on televised gladiator-style kitchen competitions like *Top Chef* and *Chopped* that pit aspiring chefs against one another. To this bloodthirsty audience, cooking has become sport, a culinary joust with winners and losers. The winners sign cookbook deals, and the losers "pack their knives and go."

But while our obsession with restaurants has grown, we haven't committed ourselves to becoming better diners. If anything, the greater lengths that restaurants go to delight us, the more complacent we've become as guests. Most of what we know about restaurants is filtered through the contrived lens of reality television or social media. Too often, ardent restaurant fans visit trendy new places to evaluate rather than to enjoy them, and crowdsourcing sites such as Yelp and Tripadvisor provide a digital community for amateur food lovers to scrutinize their dining experiences with a restaurant critic's vigor.

DINING OUT IS A SKILL, NOT A TALENT

Most people don't think of dining out as a skill—certainly not in the same way they do cooking or baking. While some people dine more gracefully than others, *no one is born a great restaurant customer.* Yet many restaurant lovers fall prey to the false assumption that dining out more imbues them with greater authority or expertise about food. You've probably dined with some of these people, the ones who spend the whole night yammering on about the merits of sous vide cooking or name-dropping which among the "World's 50 Best Restaurants" they've visited. In my experience, the people who fashion themselves the biggest experts are often the clumsiest and most entitled guests.

So, if we care so much about having great restaurant experiences, why aren't we more invested in becoming better diners? In 2014, when I founded the *Restaurant Manifesto*, my popular blog about restaurant culture, I had sensed an opportunity to encourage restaurant lovers to think differently about what it means to dine well. Every time a restaurant guest described how they liked their steak cooked in incomprehensible, abstract language such as "red but not bloody" or "medium rare to the rare side," I knew they were lacking the proper tools to communicate their needs effectively. Other guests complained that their food was horribly overcooked and under-seasoned but left nothing on the plate to justify replacing the dish or taking it off the bill. At times it drove me crazy, but I also found myself empathizing with them. Many guests simply didn't know any better.

Over the last twenty years, we've become a generation of more educated eaters, but we haven't become more educated diners. The good news is that any effort you put into becoming a more conscientious guest will repay you tenfold in more attentive service. You don't have to spend exorbitant sums of money on expensive meals to see results either. Think of it like improving your golf game. As any avid golfer knows, playing more rounds at fancy courses or buying more expensive clubs doesn't automatically improve your score. You need to work on your mechanics if you want to lower your handicap. This book focuses on improving your swing.

THE BOURDAIN EFFECT

Anthony Bourdain, the patron saint of tattooed line cooks, changed how we think about chefs by flinging open the kitchen doors and exposing the maniacal inner life of a restaurant. But as impactful as he was as a culinary shaman, he didn't do much to sharpen his readers' dining acumen, outside of telling us to avoid fish on Mondays or to skip the bacteria-infested Hollandaise at brunch. His writing gave us an unexpurgated view of the shadowy underworld of restaurants but offered few clues on how to apply those insights constructively.

Bourdain was himself the consummate diner because he loved food but also because he adored the people who cook and serve it. He said publicly that he wrote *Kitchen Confidential*, his wildly successful memoir published in 2000, for his fellow line cooks and measured its success on whether or not his kitchen comrades found the book authentic and entertaining. A quarter-century later, *Kitchen Confidential* has endured as a canonical work because Bourdain's portrait of restaurant life is so ruthlessly honest.

Before *Kitchen Confidential*, chefs were a lowly caste. After Bourdain lifted the veil on the mysterious inner workings of restaurants, chefs became edgy and cool. "The life of the cook was a life of adventure, looting, pillaging, and rock-and-rolling through life with a carefree disregard for all conventional morality," he writes. "It looked pretty darn good to me on the other side of the line." At the same time, his writing exposed many of the more nefarious aspects of restaurant life—like unsavory labor practices, mental illness, and substance abuse. He was able to convey what happens behind closed doors in restaurants with a level of candor that no other chef had ever dared before.

But beyond its influence on the restaurant community, *Kitchen Confidential* also fed the public's hunger for access. Bourdain's popular televised travelogues *Parts Unknown* and *No Reservations* turned scouring the globe in search of deliciousness into a noble pursuit. Before his shocking and sudden passing in 2018, Bourdain had become the spiritual leader to a generation of epicures, awakening them to the transformative power of food.

EVERYONE'S A CRITIC, NO ONE'S AN EXPERT

I'm always struck by how fascinated people have become with restaurants these days. At parties, I'll introduce myself to strangers with more prestigious-sounding job titles and presumably higher incomes than me, and invariably everyone will want to hear about my restaurant experience. Whether they work in law or medicine, finance, or tech, they'll pepper me with questions: *What's the worst thing a customer has done? What's the biggest tip you ever received? Do people really send back expensive bottles of wine?* If you work at a well-known restaurant, the conversation always ends the same way: *Could you help me get a reservation?*

I can't think of any subject that more random people will claim expertise about than restaurants. It's impossible to imagine myself joining a conversation of a group of accountants or lawyers and adding my two cents about tax code or bankruptcy law. But somehow whenever I start a conversation about restaurants, suddenly everyone in the room is a graduate of Le Cordon Bleu (the world-renowned French culinary school). The internet has democratized how we opine about restaurants, giving new meaning to the saying "Everyone's a critic."

Our relationship with food has changed dramatically too. We identify ourselves by our dietary choices—vegans, freegans, locavores, foragers, pescatarians, paleo, keto, low-carb, dairy-free, nut-free, or gluten-intolerant. Our food choices have become as integral to our identity as our wardrobe, hairstyle, and sexual orientation. Orthodox diets are often associated with personal growth or enlightenment. To some, a life-changing meal can lead to a shift in self-care or a more holistic view on sustainability.

Who's Who in the Dining Room

Most restaurants are divided into two distinct sectors, which are commonly referred to as the front of the house (FOH) and back of the house (BOH). The FOH includes customer-facing dining room staff, and the BOH consists of the cooks, dishwashers, porters, and other kitchen positions. Although these two hemispheres often operate independently of each other, they must work in tandem for a restaurant to perform at a high level. The FOH team is overseen by managers. Below them, waiters ("front servers" or "captains," as they're called in some fine dining restaurants) engage with guests and take orders; bussers, or "back servers," clear dishes, reset tables, and pour water; and food runners shepherd finished plates from the kitchen. Behind the bar, there is usually a main bartender, who cares for seated guests, and a "service" bartender, who prepares drinks for guests in the dining room. A barback keeps the bar supplied with clean glassware and fresh ice throughout the night and changes beer kegs when they're kicked. If the restaurant serves coffee, a barista is often responsible for preparing espresso drinks. The entrance will usually be guarded by a maître d'—short for maître d' hotel, a French term for "master of the house"—in charge of seating the restaurant, and hosts, who check coats and escort guests to their table. As with the kitchen brigade system (which I'll revisit later), FOH roles are highly specialized.

Restaurants are incubators for culinary ideas, where chefs help us contextualize our foodways and expand our palates. And while we've become more trusting of chefs over the years, we haven't developed the same trust toward the dining room staff. We're often reticent about putting blind faith in servers and bartenders, even though front-of-house staff have become more knowledgeable than ever.

Restaurant professionals are often exceedingly conscientious diners. Working in hospitality makes it impossible to dine in someone else's restaurant without showing deference to its staff. I often hear people say, "Everyone should have to work in a restaurant at least once in their life!" It's true that if everyone could walk a day in our shoes, it would dramatically change their point of view about how to behave as a diner. Hospitality professionals develop a deeper understanding of the rules of engagement in restaurants based on our experiences seeing how different guests succeed and fail at getting what they want. In other words, *we learn from your mistakes.*

ALWAYS BE YOURSELF

Approach your dining experiences with an open heart. Be honest. If you don't like something, say so. There's nothing more frustrating for a server than seeing a miserable guest conceal the cause of their discontentment. Understand that there is always more than one way to enjoy a restaurant meal. You don't have to order the dish that everyone else raves about. Order the one that speaks to you. If something goes wrong, give the staff a chance to make amends before you pass judgment. Trust that the people serving you are working in earnest to deliver the best experience for you and your guests. Never assume that every mistake is a sign of incompetence. Above all, remember that being a pleasant guest improves your chances of having a pleasant dining experience.

Later in the book, I'll discuss strategies for disarming cynicism and building solidarity with staff. Something as simple as telling your server, "We're really excited to be here!" can completely alter the trajectory of your service. These lessons will help mitigate any turbulence that you might typically encounter when interacting with waitstaff. Each chapter concludes with a takeaway, and I'll also share with you some of my favorite dining tips to keep in your back pocket for the next time you dine out—like how to tactfully request a different table, what to do when you feel rushed, and how to send food back gracefully.

Reading this book will help you become a better diner in many ways. First, it will deepen your understanding about the inner workings of restaurants. Second, you'll learn how to avoid pitfalls that might negatively affect your relationships with the people serving you. Third, you'll acquire better vocabulary that can help you more fluently communicate your needs. The journey begins with becoming a more mindful diner.

THE TAKEAWAY

Even though it seems like restaurants have been around forever, the concept of customizable dining with individualized service is still less than two centuries old. In recent decades, dining culture has accelerated at breakneck speed, and so, too, have our expectations. As diners, we get a thrill from discovering great restaurants and having transformative culinary experiences, but we don't always give enough thought to how we can become better guests. Embracing a mindset that dining is an improvable skill is critical to having more fruitful restaurant meals.

CHAPTER TWO

Becoming a More Mindful Diner

> There is a difference between dining and eating.
> Dining is an art. When you eat to get the most out of your
> meal, to please the palate, just as well as to satiate
> the appetite, that, my friend, is dining.
>
> —YUAN MEI

I was enjoying a quiet dinner alone at the bar of a bustling neighborhood restaurant in Brooklyn recently when I witnessed two women walk in shortly before closing time. While I quietly devoured the last of my fusilli pasta with duck ragu and slugged down a hearty glass of Nebbiolo, I noticed the pair out of the corner of my eye traversing the entrance, looking famished. "We don't have a reservation. Is it too late for you to feed us?" one of the women politely asked the bartender upon entering the space. "I promise we'll order quickly. We know you're closing soon."

It turns out they had no cause for worry—the kitchen was still open for another twenty minutes. But I marveled at their humility. I could see from the bartender's reaction that he appreciated it too. Another staff member scurried out from behind the service station with menus, ushering them over to a cozy corner table by the window. One of the women reiterated their promise to order quickly. You could tell they were genuinely concerned about inconveniencing the kitchen staff so close to the end of the night. I can't be sure that they had a successful meal, but the deference they showed the staff undoubtedly set them on the right path.

As a former career waiter, I can tell you that guests don't always show this level of sensitivity to the staff's needs. These women—cognizant that arriving unannounced at the end of the night might be an unwelcome development for an exhausted kitchen and waitstaff—made themselves a pleasure to serve, simply by being mindful of the circumstances. Especially on slow nights, hours might go by in a restaurant without a single party walking through the door. So, when a group saunters in five minutes before closing expecting a multiple course meal with cocktails and wine, it can be demoralizing. For tipped employees, the extra time spent serving one late table dilutes their hourly earnings by prolonging the shift without adding any significant income.

Hospitality purists will argue that restaurants should be welcoming toward every guest who walks in the door no matter what time they arrive, provided that it's during advertised business hours. They'll say, "The restaurant shouldn't stay open until midnight if they don't want to serve the people who walk in at 11:55 p.m.!" In their minds, hospitality should be extended unconditionally from the moment the doors open to the moment they close. "If the staff doesn't like it, they should find another job." And while the restaurant owner may agree with this sentiment, the owner also isn't the person stuck serving one table until 2:00 a.m. in an empty dining room.

Rather than insisting that every customer has the right to show up five minutes before closing time and occupy a table indefinitely, diners should be mindful not to wear out their welcome when they arrive late. If you don't have a reservation, you should try to arrive at least thirty minutes before a restaurant's scheduled closing time to avoid a situation where you're holding an entire staff hostage just to serve your table. If you sit down less than thirty minutes before the restaurant closes, be willing to order right away so you aren't detaining the kitchen staff longer than necessary.

One of the biggest mistakes people make when they dine out is approaching restaurant experiences too passively. As guests, we're conditioned to think that the joy of dining outside of our homes is rooted in absolving ourselves of responsibility for cooking, cleaning, or hosting. Of course, this is integral to the pleasure, but a restaurant experience shouldn't feel like relaxing on a massage table. It's nice to feel pampered, but what makes restaurant experiences so unique and special is that they're interactive.

In his seminal book *Setting the Table,* the hospitality guru Danny Meyer, who founded Union Square Hospitality Group in New York City and the fast casual burger chain Shake Shack, draws a smart distinction between service and hospitality. "Service is a monologue," he writes. "Hospitality, on the other hand, is a *dialogue.*" In his view, hospitality is meant to be *shared* with guests, not administered to them. To be successful, he stresses the need to cultivate a sense of "shared ownership" with guests. But even though Meyer's brand of "enlightened hospitality" purports to put employees first, it underplays the guest's role in fostering healthy hospitality dialogues. I can say from experience that when guests aren't invested and engaged, it's more difficult for staff to deliver successful outcomes.

In *Setting the Table,* Meyer preaches about the transformative nature of hospitality. But his vision for achieving that transformation is often one-sided. "It may seem implicit in the philosophy of enlightened hospitality that the employee is constantly setting aside personal needs and selflessly taking care of others," writes Meyer. "But the real secret of its success is to hire people to whom caring for others is, in fact, a selfish act." In other words, Meyer regards his special sauce as recruiting staff who believe that overcompensating for guests' shortcomings, when necessary, should be considered a pleasure, provided that it's in the interest of delivering great service. But to me, genuine hospitality— the animated exchange between server and guest—is a two-way street, where mindful guests are willing to meet their servers halfway without feeling inconvenienced.

A NEW WAY OF THINKING ABOUT RESTAURANT SERVICE

There is nothing inherently wrong with Danny Meyer's enlightened approach to hospitality. Centering customers' needs is essential to the success of any service-oriented business, and Meyer deserves credit for helping to legitimize restaurant work as a viable career path. But I advocate embracing a new mindset toward restaurant experiences in which guests take more ownership of their role in fostering positive dynamics at the table. The truth is: in most real-life hospitality scenarios, the staff is simply meeting people where they are. This shouldn't mean that they're unwilling to go the extra mile when guests are passive and disengaged. It simply means that the guests' energy often sets the tone for how far the staff will go.

Meyer might say that meeting people where they are is insufficient and that great service should supersede any deficiencies that guests bring to the table. In his mind, if a guest had a terrible day, great servers should shower them with even more kindness to reverse their sullen mood. In a perfect world, every server would have an unlimited reservoir of generosity to bestow upon every guest who needs extra love, but restaurants do not exist in a perfect world. Servers are human beings who have bad days too.

The reality is that when you dine in a restaurant, your service largely reflects your energy at the table. If you come across as disinterested when a server enthusiastically greets you, they may assume that you'd prefer to be left alone. But if you respond with genuine interest, it can help sustain the server's excitement and friendliness. Truly enlightened hospitality, in my view, goes both ways, and we should never expect staff to deliver warmth when it isn't reciprocated.

BEING PRESENT IS MORE IMPORTANT
THAN BEING NICE

Any experienced waiter will tell you: the most pleasant guests to take care of in a restaurant are not always the nicest ones. Anyone can be polite by rote, but the best guests are the most attentive, patient, and compliant ones. Saying please and thank you is always appreciated, of course, but servers don't need guests to shower them with pleasantries. They need people to pay attention and respect the rules.

Being present in a restaurant is not as easy as it once was. Enjoying a two-hour dinner free of digital distractions feels like a heavy lift, but keeping your smartphone in your pocket or purse can pay dividends. Guests who are glued to their phones while a waiter struggles to command their attention may receive less attentive service. Unless you need to have your phone out—for personal or work-related emergencies—then put it away. You're far less likely to alienate your server if you aren't constantly on your phone watching Instagram videos.

When guests are more present at the table, they can foster stronger connections with staff without virtue signaling. Believe it or not, there are times when restaurant customers can be *too friendly*. Showing interest in a server's personal life or pursuits outside of work, for example, can backfire and make the server feel awkward. *Never* ask the dreaded question: "What else do you do outside of the restaurant?" It drives waiters crazy because it implies that waiting tables alone is not a serious pursuit.

Some diners think that peppering their server with personal questions is a way to build solidarity. But questions like "Where did you grow up?" or "What other restaurants have you worked in?" can feel intrusive, even threatening, if the server doesn't feel comfortable with the established rapport. When I waited tables, it always bothered me when guests would ask my name before I introduced myself, especially when they didn't share theirs in return. If you insist on asking your server their name, always tell them yours first. In my opinion, it's also best to wait until you've developed a relationship organically with your server before you start asking personal questions.

TREAT EVERY RESTAURANT
LIKE SOMEONE'S HOME

Most restaurants—especially family-owned, independent ones—are born from deeply personal origin stories. They might inhabit historic spaces, be named in honor of relatives who inspired a love of cooking, and be passed down through generations. Their menus often reflect a chef's personal journey of culinary discovery. I once interviewed a restaurateur who'd purchased several animal statues from a defunct Rainforest Café because he and his wife had one of their first dates there. After reclaiming the animals, he found hidden spaces in his own restaurant to display them as an homage to the couple's personal history.

Even though restaurants are communal spaces open to the public, they should always be treated with the same respect as someone's home. If a new acquaintance invites you over to their house, you wouldn't randomly rearrange furniture to make yourself more comfortable or start making demands about what they should serve for dinner. Likewise, you shouldn't push tables together or move chairs around in a restaurant without asking permission first. If you lose your napkin, don't swipe a clean one from the perfectly set table next to you. Politely ask a server to bring you a fresh one, the same as you would if you were a guest in someone's home and needed something.

When restaurants refuse to rearrange chairs and tables to accommodate your seating preferences, it's often to keep their homes in order. Management understands the physical limitations of their spaces better than guests do, and they know how reconfiguring the floor plan can disrupt traffic patterns by crowding aisles or blocking entryways. Occasionally, making one guest more comfortable jeopardizes another guest's comfort—like allowing a late-arriving guest to squeeze into a banquette that is shared with a neighboring table. One party might be thrilled that the restaurant made space for their friend, but the neighboring couple sharing a romantic evening might suddenly feel crowded.

In the revised centennial edition of Emily Post's *Etiquette* published in 2022, her great-great-grandchildren wisely write: "When dining out, the goal is to have a wonderful time, but not at the expense of others." Restaurants have become so adept at catering to every guest's individual needs that sometimes it's easy to forget that we're dining in a room full of other people. A great restaurant makes you feel like yours is the only table. But for restaurant workers, keeping a dining room filled with people happy is a complicated puzzle in which the pieces rarely fit together easily.

Danny Meyer describes the complex machinations behind running a restaurant in *Setting the Table:* "A restaurant has all kinds of moving parts that make it particularly challenging. In order to succeed, you need to apply—simultaneously—exceptional skills in selecting real estate, negotiating, hiring, training, motivating, purchasing, budgeting, designing, manufacturing, cooking, tasting, pricing, selling, servicing, marketing, and hosting." Every successful dining experience is the product of a staff's tireless work, for which their ultimate goal is to ensure that every table leaves happy.

But Newton's law is a powerful force in restaurants. Every action creates an equal or opposite reaction. At one table, a toddler is deathly allergic to tree nuts, so the kitchen needs to be checked for cross-contamination. The precious minutes it takes to sterilize surfaces and utensils may cause another table's food to be delayed. A party of high rollers spills a three-hundred-dollar bottle of Bordeaux all over their table and wants it replaced right away, which makes the sommelier late arriving to another table, a couple needing help with the wine list. Unexpected circumstances arise every night. Someone orders a kosher meal that was supposed to be delivered from a different restaurant, and no one in the kitchen knows who took in the delivery or its whereabouts. A private party of forty teenagers who just came from a Taylor Swift concert is squealing so loudly that other guests are complaining, but the birthday girl's father is an investor, so the managers are disinclined to ask the group to quiet down. In the history of the restaurant business, there has never been a dining room filled with only well-behaved, polite, and patient guests.

If chefs could cook as though the restaurant only had one table, they could easily accommodate every special request. But that's not how restaurants work. Kitchen systems are designed to be routine and repeatable. Like the industrialized factories that inspired it, the brigade system evolved out of the need for consistency in a professional kitchen. Line cooks are trained to execute highly specified tasks that rely on muscle memory. Anything that could potentially disrupt the flow increases the probability that systems will break down and mistakes will be made.

The Brigade System

The modern brigade system, an innovation widely credited to the French chef Auguste Escoffier in the late nineteenth century, laid the foundation for modern restaurant cooking. In these brigades, labor is divided to maximize efficiency, speed, and consistency like a factory assembly line. They operate with a rigid hierarchy of leadership reminiscent of a military organization in which tasks are compartmentalized among a team of line cooks. In old-school French brigades, chefs often wore toques—or tall, cylindrical hats—that would traditionally indicate a chef's rank. The taller the toque a chef wears, the higher their rank. Line cooks typically start in the prep kitchen, then graduate to positions with greater responsibility such as *garde manger* (the "pantry chef" who prepares salads and cold appetizers), *grillardin* (the grill chef), *saucier* (the sauté chef, also in charge of making sauces), or *tournant* (a versatile position that fills in as needed). Eventually, a talented cook may rise to the rank of *sous-chef,* the most senior lieutenant to the *chef de cuisine,* who oversees the kitchen's day-to-day operations.

Menus also need to be streamlined for speed and precision. Chefs are often forced to make sacrifices with their own culinary vision for the sake of operational efficiency, especially in high-volume restaurants. When the chef insists on having the table's order all at once—as opposed to allowing the table to order appetizers and main courses piecemeal—it's because the kitchen can't handle allowing *every* table in the restaurant to order that way without causing systems to break down.

LEND A HELPING HAND WHERE YOU CAN

Lately, I've been noticing how rarely my dining companions make an effort to assist servers with their work, whether it be helping to clear a plate from a hard-to-reach area on the table or adjusting the position of an empty glass to make it easier for servers to refill or remove it. Staff appreciates when guests acknowledge their efforts by offering to lend a hand now and then. These small acts of goodwill require minimal effort, but a simple gesture such as placing a serving spoon on a dirty plate before it's cleared can make a significant impact on how servers perceive you.

It isn't necessary to take this to the extreme. Servers can be annoyed when overly eager guests try too hard to be their "helpers." What's most important is becoming more cognizant of the staff's movements and body language. If a server is a struggling to place a side dish in the middle of the table for sharing, for example, a mindful guest will offer to take the plate from them and set it down themselves. Whenever you can make the staff's life easier by removing an obstacle or clearing a path for them to deliver smoother service, it demonstrates that you see yourself as a partner, not just a patron.

BE AN ENTHUSIASTIC TABLE TURNER

The most enlightened guests are always respectful about how long they occupy their table. Although restaurants have become a bit stricter in recent years, most still don't set rigid parameters about when they need tables back because doing so risks making guests feel unwelcome. But the economics of restaurants are changing, and tighter profit margins place added pressure on businesses to serve more guests in less time.

"Turning tables"—the industry term for getting parties in and out in a timely manner—has become essential to maximizing revenue and profitability.

It isn't always easy to control the pacing and keep people moving, but skilled waiters are able to shepherd guests swiftly through their meals without making them feel rushed. In busy restaurants, managers are maniacal about turn times because shorter turns mean greater productivity. Most of the time when your server gently nudges you about ordering another drink or solicits your dessert order before you've had time to consider, it's usually a veiled attempt to move your table along as quickly as possible. Don't take it personally. Turning tables expeditiously is a necessary aspect of running a healthy restaurant business.

Bear in mind that when a restaurant charges a certain price, say thirty-five dollars for a main course, that price is based on certain assumptions about how many guests the restaurant can serve per night and the average time allotted for each table. With fewer guests and longer turn times, restaurants need to raise prices. It is not a coincidence that the most expensive restaurants in the world have only one or two seatings per night. When someone pays upward of five hundred dollars a head for a meal, they're paying for the privilege of dining at their own pace. But restaurants with more moderate prices can't afford to give guests the same leeway.

When I waited tables, I used to love when guests would say, "Let us know if you need the table back" (unless they were being passive-aggressive about it, of course). It's a great habit to get into if you're finishing up your meal and you see a crowd at the bar. If you've already paid your check, there's a very good chance that your table is needed right away. Showing sensitivity about returning the table demonstrates that you understand your role in supporting a restaurant's financial health. Conversely, earning a reputation for monopolizing tables can jeopardize your ability to secure future reservations. If you're enjoying yourself and don't want to leave, ask a staff member if they could help relocate your party to the bar. If the restaurant does need the table back, they'll be delighted to move you and might even offer to buy everyone a round of drinks for being so considerate.

I once worked as a captain in a very exclusive cocktail bar with only four tables, where I was also responsible for managing the reservation manifest and plotting the seating chart. With only four tables, it was essential that every table turn as quickly as possible. The jewel box–like space had no comfortable waiting area, which meant that if anyone arrived late in the first seating or if tables were slow to order, the consequences would be devastating later in the night. Generally, parties of two were allotted an hour and a half per seating, four-tops would be given two hours, and parties of six or more two and a half to three hours. The slightest disruption to one table's timing would wreak havoc on the flow of service and our ability to seat everyone punctually.

Every restaurant has its own template for booking tables and keeping the dining room full. But it's an imperfect science. No matter how technologically advanced the reservation software is, no system can possibly predict which tables will be on time and which won't or how long every table plans to stay. Some parties are old friends that haven't seen each other forever, so they linger; others are businesspeople who'd prefer to eat quickly before their long evening commute. A couple could be out having a romantic dinner to celebrate their tenth anniversary, or they might be two strangers on a miserable blind date. The lovebirds may occupy the table for over three hours, while the Tinder situation falls apart before the main courses arrive. As the gatekeeper, the maître d' has one of the hardest jobs in the restaurant. They must nimbly adapt to these constantly changing circumstances to make sure every guest is seated on time and table waits are minimized.

No one likes waiting for their table in a restaurant. But with so many unpredictable variables, occasional waits are unavoidable. Showing grace when you have to wait a half-hour for a table when you had a reservation isn't easy. I've seen customers throw tantrums like bed-wetting toddlers after being seated just fifteen minutes past their reservation time. I understand that it's frustrating to be trapped in a crowded bar with nowhere to sit, waiting for a table, but in densely populated cities like New York, where space is always at a premium, a restaurant can only do so much with its own spatial limitations.

If a long wait is an isolated incident and not a chronic problem, then it should be accepted graciously up to thirty minutes with minimal blowback. But always keep in mind that a protracted wait, in most cases, simply means that the restaurant's reservation plan didn't play out as expected. The root cause of the delays may be tardiness, kitchen problems, or slow table turns, but any of these issues has the potential to create a domino effect that causes a pileup at the door.

This is why when you arrive more than fifteen minutes late for your reservation, the host or maître d' may well deliver a sharp invective about needing you to return the table at a specific time. Respecting those wishes shows that you accept responsibility for putting the restaurant in an uncompromising position. Some may argue that it's inhospitable to make demands on returning the table simply because someone got stuck in traffic or had a family emergency, but the reality is that the whole reservation system can break down if every late guest is given clemency.

If the same person showed up thirty minutes late to the doctor's office or hair salon, they would likely have to reschedule their appointment. But for some reason, most diners expect restaurants to honor their reservations if they arrive significantly past their assigned time. Obviously, a restaurant meal on average takes more time than a haircut, but the time is relative. Neither should be rushed. The fact is: you simply cannot run any appointment-based business that tolerates tardiness without serious repercussions. Because restaurants are a hospitality-driven business, some customers expect leniency, but there's really no reason they should be treated any differently than when they're late for a medical appointment or a salon visit.

MANAGING EXPECTATIONS
AND QUIETING YOUR INNER CRITIC

These days, many diners expect restaurant meals to be life-changing, but I think we should expect them to be *life-affirming*. It's easy to understand why people have such elevated expectations: if they only have one chance to enjoy a meal somewhere exclusive, they want that experience to live up to the hype, if not exceed it. If you're traveling overseas and visiting a world-famous restaurant such as Noma in Copenhagen or Disfrutar in Barcelona, knowing that you may never be able to return, you want the experience to be mind-blowing.

But when diners approach restaurant experiences with overblown expectations, they could be setting themselves up to be disappointed. Visiting a restaurant with the mindset of evaluating its worth rather than enjoying its charms makes it less likely that guests will be open to having an immersive experience. I don't begrudge anyone for having strong opinions about food, but scrutinizing every meal like a restaurant critic takes the fun out of dining.

I'm always amused when I hear underwhelmed diners say things like "The fish was good, but I can make it better at home." What makes remarks like this so absurd is that professional chefs don't cook like people do at home. As I described earlier, restaurant kitchens are designed to produce flavorful food at scale, which involves serving large groups of people simultaneously. If you think you can make the same dish better at home, imagine having to cook ten different versions with random modifications—no oil, light on the salt, sauce on the side—and having to make sure that each one comes out hot and perfectly seasoned in less than fifteen minutes. Then you have to do it all over again for eight hours straight without a break. It probably wouldn't be so easy then, would it?

NOTHING YOU ASK FOR IN A RESTAURANT IS EVER EASY

You get a lot of peculiar requests working in restaurants. I've had grown adults ask me to cut their meat into tiny bites because they just had dental surgery and are having difficulty chewing. Some people are so serious about how they like their martinis prepared that they design special cards with printed instructions to give to bartenders when they sit down. In hospitality, you do your best to accommodate even the most exotic requests, but making people happy can be exhausting.

Whenever you ask for something out of the ordinary in a restaurant, no matter how small the request, it has the potential to disrupt service. Even something as simple as asking for a side of mustard can be challenging. If mustard isn't part of the kitchen's mise en place (the line cooks' regimented assemblage of prepared ingredients), then someone will have to retrieve the container of mustard from the walk-in cooler, which is typically in an entirely different part of the restaurant. That person will then have to stop what they're doing, leave their place in the kitchen, grab the large tub of mustard from the walk-in, find a ramekin, spoon out the mustard, and then return the container to the fridge. In the precious minutes it takes them to deliver the mustard, unattended tasks can begin to pile up.

If you embrace the idea that nothing in a restaurant is easy, then you shouldn't ever be disappointed when a restaurant can't accommodate a special request. Mindful guests are willing to respect the rules without feeling entitled to special treatment. They usually understand without convincing that whenever a restaurant says no, it's a decision that was reached after careful deliberation, not the will of a vindictive chef or inhospitable management. Restaurants have no incentive to deny customers what they want, but unfortunately, pleasing every guest on their own terms isn't always practical. It helps when diners accept this reality.

EVERY RESTAURANT IS DIFFERENT

It's very hard to generalize about how one should behave in every restaurant because not every restaurant experience is the same. How guests should comport themselves during a sixteen-course tasting menu at a Michelin-starred restaurant is different from how they should behave in their local Irish pub having a burger and a pint of Guinness. While certain rules of engagement such as being attentive to staff and tipping generously are universal, there may be less pressure to adhere to other ground rules; for example, ordering appetizers separately from entrées or expecting your party to be seated incomplete are usually more acceptable when you're dining in a casual chain restaurant versus a more formal place. A mindful diner can carefully calibrate their behavior to properly fit the setting.

It's always wise to take stock of the room whenever you enter a new restaurant. Finding cues in the environment can often help you determine the proper level of formality. Take note of the table settings. Are there fine linen tablecloths and napkins that have been neatly folded, or is the table covered with a layer of disposable paper and silverware roll-ups? How is the staff dressed? Are the managers wearing business suits and dresses? Do the servers have on jeans with branded T-shirts and white aprons? Fine dining restaurants are dressing down these days, but uniforms still say a lot about whether a dining experience is meant to be casual or formal.

Bear in mind that a more casual setting isn't necessarily an invitation to be boisterous, not any more than a formal environment should discourage guests from letting loose and having a good time. In a formal setting, it might be more appropriate to defer to the house rules, whereas in a casual setting, it may be more acceptable to bend them. Either way, a mindful guest will be aware of the environment inside a restaurant and align their behavior accordingly.

THE TAKEAWAY

In the hospitality field, waiters are taught: "Think of yourself as a guest." But it helps when guests are willing to think of themselves as waiters too. Memorable restaurant experiences result from a profound connection between staff and guests, and that bond is easier to achieve when both parties are engaged and present. For restaurant experiences to reach their full potential, diners must be active participants. There is no sense in sitting back and waiting for sparks to fly as a guest when you can set the fires yourself.

CHAPTER THREE

ℬe a 𝒫articipant, 𝒩ot a 𝒮pectator

A good restaurant is like a vacation. It transports you, and
it becomes a lot more than just about the food.
—PHIL ROSENTHAL

If you were dining at the opulent Café Mécanique in Paris in 1786, you
would be seated at a luxurious marble table perched above long hollow
columns that feed directly down to the kitchen below. After the maître d'
places your order through a voice tube embedded underneath the table,
the food ascends like magic through an intricate pulley system. Appar-
ently, Thomas Jefferson was so charmed by what he saw during a visit
to Café Mécanique that he had a similar dumbwaiter system installed
in his Monticello estate in Virginia.

The spectacle created by the automated tables at Café Mécanique
was remarkably prescient. It illustrated a truth about dining out that
remains true today: restaurants are a form of living theater. Centuries
later, incorporating stagecraft into dining experiences would become
increasingly common in modern restaurants. When sushi chef and in-
novator Yoshiaki Shiraishi, inspired by a visit to a beer bottling factory
in Osaka, developed the technology behind sushi conveyor belt restaurants in 1958, he believed the innovation would breathe new life (and
efficiency) into the static counter service found in traditional sushi bars.
He was right. By the early 2000s, there were over twenty-seven hundred
conveyor belt sushi restaurants across Japan.

We've seen this type of spectacle echoed in the dramatic flourishes at restaurants like Aureole in Las Vegas, where the iconic "Wine Angel," a server in a shimmering bodysuit, launches skyward on a hidden harness to retrieve wine bottles from the towering walls of a vertical wine cellar, and in the jungle-themed absurdity of the Rainforest Café, where guests dine against a backdrop of animatronic wildlife and simulated thunderstorms. The more the dining public relies on restaurants for diversion, the more restaurants have become entertainment venues.

In the past few decades, table-side theatrics have made a comeback in fine dining restaurants, with nostalgic touches like flambé desserts and roving prime rib carts in vogue again. We can also see the thirst for spectacle reflected in the attention-grabbing feats of molecular gastronomy, like the smoke-filled cloches and isomalt balloons being paraded through the dining room at Alinea in Chicago, where chef Grant Achatz and his team splatter-paint sauces directly onto each table for their dessert course like edible Jackson Pollack paintings.

But the allure of eighteenth-century Parisian restaurants went beyond the theatrical nature of their physical spaces. As with restaurants today, the real theater was in the people watching. In *Dining Out: A Global History of Restaurants*, Katie Lawson and Elliott Shore describe an anachronistic scene at Café Mécanique reminiscent of the clubby vibes inside many of today's trendiest hotspots. "The spectacle of the Café Mécanique was not only the automation, but the attendant crowd," they write. "Seeing and being seen were at the heart of restaurant dining in the late eighteenth and early nineteenth-century Paris." Restaurants have always been prime locations for people watching.

Rebecca Spang echoes the sentiment in her book *The Invention of the Restaurant: Paris and Modern Gastronomic Culture*. She notes how nineteenth-century restaurants in Paris provided an escape, where diners could lose themselves in the ambience and energy of the room. "Restaurants were places of daydream and fantasy," she writes, "places to tell tales of who the other patrons were and who one was oneself." From the earliest incarnations of Parisian restaurants, the spectacle was already integral to their allure. Much like restaurant audiences do today, nineteenth-century French diners didn't just come to eat; they also came to enjoy the show. "Like a theater," Spang notes, "a restaurant was a stable frame around an ever-changing performance, a stage where fantasies might be brought to life."

Chef Auguste Escoffier and his business partner César Ritz (of Ritz-Carlton fame) saw the appeal of designing ostentatious settings for wealthy clientele to dine out in the lap of luxury. Their partnership in London's cosmopolitan Savoy Hotel in 1890 would be considered contemporary by today's standards. A guest dining in their restaurant would find many of the same accents and amenities one sees today in elegant dining rooms across the world—servers outfitted in bespoke formal wear, fine threaded table linens, elaborate floral designs, and dramatic mood lighting. The pioneering duo understood that the key to designing a successful restaurant was creating something uniquely experiential, as appealing to the eyes as it was to the palate. Over a century ago, restaurants were already creating Instagrammable moments to delight their guests.

The legacy of theatrical dining continued throughout the twentieth century, during which it began to take on a more familiar shape as modern gastronomy evolved in America. Henri Soulé's Le Pavillon arrived in New York City in 1941, when French cuisine was considered the gold standard of fine dining. (A temporary outpost of Le Pavillon had been in residence at the 1939 World's Fair in Queens before the restaurant moved into its permanent location in Midtown Manhattan.) Soulé understood how dramatic embellishments like table-side service and bountiful chef's buffets overflowing with caviar and chilled shellfish injected adrenaline into the dining room.

The interior of Joe Baum's iconic Four Seasons Restaurant—which entered the pantheon of opulent New York City dining rooms in 1959—still stands as a marvel of midcentury architecture. The Philip Johnson–designed interior, with its towering ceilings, warm French walnut walls, suspended bronze sculptures, and shimmering chain-link window dressings, provided a dramatic backdrop for a meal and redefined how modern restaurants look and feel. Its popularity as a dining destination and its reputation as the birthplace of the "power lunch" (the kind we see depicted in TV shows like *Mad Men* and *Billions*) is inextricable from the palatial environs, a setting that makes its occupants feel important simply for having a table there.

Restaurants today are still places to see and be seen. Pick up any tabloid newspaper, and its celebrity sightings will invariably mention the buzzy restaurant where Beyoncé or Taylor Swift were photographed sneaking in for dinner. The openness of a restaurant setting makes it the perfect proscenium for human drama, providing endless thrills for desperate oglers looking for a glimpse into the private lives of the rich and famous. Developing a reputation for attracting celebrities can extend the lifespan of a restaurant more than any number of Michelin stars ever could.

WE LIKE TO DINE,
BUT WE LOVE TO WATCH

It's easy to draw a line from the pomp and circumstance of Le Pavillon and the Four Seasons directly to the amusement park atmosphere of some of today's most flamboyant restaurants. At Papi Steak, a clubby chophouse in Miami, a $1,000 Wagyu ribeye is escorted to the table by a squadron of boisterous servers carrying a gold briefcase studded with diamonds. When they open the case, a bright-yellow light glows from inside (designed to emulate the opening scene in the movie *Pulp Fiction*), and the prized cut of raw beef emerges from under a cloud of smoke. To signify its arrival, the steak has its own designated entrance music, which blares from the speakers until the procession arrives. The frenzy reaches its peak when a besuited manager brandishes a cattle prod–like instrument and singes the words *Papi Steak* into the meat, before it's ushered back to the kitchen for grilling. Escoffier's adoring guests in 1897 were likely similarly awestruck by the cherries jubilee he flambéed in honor of Queen Victoria's Diamond Jubilee.

Today's diners expect deliciousness, but they also expect to come away with some social media capital. As guests, we discharge our cell phone cameras in restaurants with the reverie of a rock concert, rather than with the reverence of a quiet theater. Most Broadway theaters forbid audience members from using their phones during the performance, so as not to disturb the actors. It's revealing that no such graces are expected of restaurant audiences, who are allowed to capture as many digital souvenirs as they want without worrying how the disruption might affect the performance.

The concert mentality makes sense. Celebrity chefs today are treated like rockstars, and scoring tables at their restaurants can be as hard to come by as a ticket for Rhianna's latest tour. Some high-end restaurants like Alinea in Chicago have taken to selling tickets online in lieu of reservations, underlining the fact that these dining experiences are more than just a meal. You're attending an event.

No one has better exemplified the zeitgeist of the modern celebrity chef and social media showman over the last decade than the Turkish steak whisperer Nusret Gökçe, lustfully known by his viral alter ego "Salt Bae." After a 2017 video of him seductively slicing meat in a skin-tight tank top was shared over fifteen million times, Gökçe became internationally known and proceeded to open personally branded steakhouses all around the world. Fans continue to flock to his restaurants, from Beverly Hills to London to Dubai, hoping to catch a glimpse of his signature table-side christening of salt, which he delivers with a flick of the wrist over an obscenely expensive dry aged tomahawk steak sheathed in 24-karat gold leaf. While diners are often awestruck by the spectacle a restaurant offers, many have also become so distracted with documenting every element of the experience on their phones that they forget to enjoy the food.

The smartphone, perhaps more than any other technological innovation in history, has changed the way we dine. Having the ability not only to capture and chronicle our dining experiences but to broadcast them digitally in real time has created a virtual realm for us to share our culinary discoveries with others. But the distraction of living on our phones has drawbacks too. Often, we wall ourselves into these digital worlds where we become more attuned to the spectacle of a restaurant than to the restaurant experience itself. No matter how many social media followers you have, taking selfies with a triple-decker shellfish tower will never be as much fun as eating it.

The Phone Eats First

Years ago, I was working as a brand ambassador for a New York–based restaurant company that opened a franchise of one of its flagship restaurants in Hong Kong. While living and working there, I noticed that many of our local guests took detailed photographs of their food before eating it. Of course, this was common in New York, too, but in Hong Kong, they seemed to take the assignment much more seriously. I'd watch with amusement as a six-top of twenty-somethings would stand up and crowd the table like paparazzi to capture as much footage of their food being delivered as possible. One of the waiters, a Hong Kong native, taught me a local Cantonese saying that, loosely translated, means: "The phone (or camera) eats first." The phrase was meant facetiously because so many people in Hong Kong, especially the younger generation, were obsessed with capturing the nuances of every meal with their cell phones and broadcasting them to their social media followers.

For their part, restaurants have had to fundamentally change the way they serve their guests—in some cases even reimagining entire concepts—because of how ubiquitous cell phone cameras have become in the dining room. While viral figures like Salt Bae might fade from the public consciousness and into obscurity, the continued proliferation of viral food trends on social media signifies that the spectacle of dining is fueling public interest in restaurants more than ever.

MAKE MEMORIES, NOT CONTENT

One night, while discussing the menu with a well-dressed group of university students in Hong Kong, a soft-spoken young man in his early twenties asked me, "Which one of your dishes is the most photogenic?" I paused to process exactly what he was asking, then responded with properly calibrated New York sassiness: "Are you only planning to take pictures of your food, or are you going to eat it too?" He chuckled nervously, but I could tell that he was being serious. I tried not to be too judgmental. Posting photos of his meals on social media was important to him, and he wanted to make sure his followers were treated to the most appetizing images.

Eventually, I answered his question as seriously as I could, but looking back, the experience reminded me how often diners prioritize aesthetics over flavor—seeking out the most Instagrammable dishes instead of the items that they're going to enjoy eating the most. I understand that beautiful restaurant food makes great content. But our need to document every food experience can border on compulsion, so that whenever we dine somewhere special, we feel obliged to capture archival footage of everything we ate. The problem arises when turning food into content becomes an obstacle to enjoying the restaurant experience itself.

I often find myself rolling my eyes at the sight of gastro-tourists incessantly photographing their food with their iPhones or influencers walking into a restaurant with ring lights and camera accessories. But all cynicism aside, restaurants would likely never have become the cultural juggernauts they are today without the power of digital media. This can be both a blessing and a curse. A blessing when it encourages culinary discovery, such as when we use social media to eavesdrop on our friends' latest meal in Japan or when we consult with our favorite local food personalities on Instagram to find out which hot places are worth the hype. A curse when we use it to fetishize restaurants and develop unhealthy obsessions with the daily habits of food influencers.

LEAVE YOUR PHONE IN YOUR POCKET

One of my favorite food writers, Jaya Saxena, penned a missive for *Eater* in 2024 about the scourge of food influencers deploying LED lights in dimly lit restaurants to achieve the perfect money shot to broadcast on their socials. "When making a reservation, you consent to being a part of the business of the restaurant, paying what's necessary and acting in a way that doesn't disrupt those around you," writes Saxena. "In exchange, you receive a meal and also all that hospitality brings. You do not consent to suddenly becoming a studio audience."

In early 2024, Frog Club, a trendy new restaurant in New York City's West Village (that has since closed), made a big splash with its controversial cell phone policy; the restaurant required patrons to surrender their phones upon arrival, after which a staff member would cover the camera aperture with black tape. As you might imagine, the policy rubbed many guests the wrong way. But, at least initially, the controversy only seemed to add to the restaurant's mystique.

When smartphone technology first arrived in the early aughts, many upscale restaurants had firm policies prohibiting laptop computers in the dining room. An illuminated computer screen is discourteous to others, and back then, restaurant managers would often need to approach guests to ask them to stow their laptops. But cell phone use is much harder to regulate. Because smartphones have become so ubiquitous, it's almost impossible for restaurants to set rigid rules about how patrons can use them in the dining room.

But mindful guests should still adhere to basic common courtesy when using cell phones at the table. At a minimum, make sure your phone is set to silent mode. Try to avoid deploying your camera flash when using your phone to take photographs or video. If you have to send a text or email, position your phone below table level to limit the light exposure. Also, avoid constantly resting your phone on the tabletop, as the space may be needed for servers to deliver cocktails and plates of food or to replenish your silverware.

LOSE YOURSELF IN THE MOMENT

The overarching goal of hospitality is to provide an immersive experience for guests, an escape from everyday life filled with scrumptious food and welcoming service. Restaurants go to great lengths to minimize distractions. We pore over every detail—the lighting fixtures, the temperature of the room, the eclectic playlist. But it's increasingly difficult to properly calibrate the atmosphere with the constant distraction of flashing cell phone screens detracting from the ambience.

Every server knows the frustration of trying to command a table's attention when guests are distracted by their phones. It poisons the lines of communication. Servers end up having to repeat themselves because guests aren't listening. Inevitably, someone ends up missing pertinent information about the menu, which can lead them to order a dish with an ingredient they don't like.

At the end of the day, the encroachment of technology has driven a wedge between what guests want and what restaurants are trying to do. Restaurants want their guests to feel fully engaged in the experience, but it's increasingly difficult to create an immersive world when so many guests are distracted by their phones. The only way that guests can become truly involved in a restaurant experience is to filter out as many of their own digital distractions as possible.

THE TAKEAWAY

It may seem counterintuitive, but when you dine out, you should lean in, rather than leaning back. The joy of a restaurant experience lies in spontaneous interactions and unexpected surprises. You should never be a passive participant or simply an audience. Think of your role more like a character in a live theater piece. To truly enjoy a restaurant, you should always feel like you're *in* the show, not simply watching it.

CHAPTER FOUR

Trusting Your Own Instincts

We all eat, and it would be a sad waste
of opportunity to eat badly.

—ANNA THOMAS

When I worked at a well-known Italian American restaurant in New York City, the captains often joked behind the scenes about guests who regularly ordered the "Number One." The Number One meant the table ordered only the restaurant's famous dishes, or its greatest hits, without even looking at the menu. Guests would bundle the components of their order like a combo meal at McDonald's: a Caesar salad to start, spicy rigatoni with meatballs on the side, and a veal parmesan. The staff understood perfectly well why everybody ordered the Number One; the dishes that came with it were the most popular items on the menu, and they were all delicious. But it was almost comical how many guests who dined with us had predetermined what they were going to order before they sat down. After a while, I found it depressing that so many other wonderful dishes on the menu were being routinely ignored.

When most diners visit a restaurant for the first time, they want to experience the best it has to offer. Many international travelers only have one opportunity to experience a restaurant in a foreign city. So they want to make that visit count. It's totally understandable if someone is spending hundreds, if not thousands, of dollars on one meal that they might not feel so inclined to take risks with their order. But by the same token, I gathered from reading online reviews of the restaurant where I worked that quite a few people who ordered the Number One left unimpressed,

48

feeling that the restaurant wasn't worth the hype or that it was over-priced for dishes you could have in any red sauce joint in Little Italy for half the price. After reading all these negative takes, I couldn't help wondering whether the Number One was simply the wrong order for certain people. What would've happened if those people had been more open to ordering something else?

Be honest: how many times have you been to a restaurant that everyone else raves about and, after having a mediocre meal, you leave wondering why it gets so much hype? Similarly, how many times have you ordered a restaurant's "signature dish" and wondered why it has such a stellar reputation? Diners often feel obligated to order a restaurant's most well-known dishes, the ones they see posted all over Instagram and TikTok, but then they're let down when these dishes don't live up to the hype. The internet can be a valuable resource for information about restaurants, but it can also encourage groupthink, making diners more inclined to follow the herd than to trust their own preferences.

KEEP YOUR RESEARCH TO A MINIMUM

It's hard to believe that there was a time not so long ago when it was impossible to know what was on a restaurant's menu without walking into the physical restaurant and holding it in your hands. Today we can browse menus from virtually any restaurant in the world on our mobile phones. We can peruse reviews, scour photographs of the food, and sift through amateur opinions about what dishes are must-haves. In anticipation of a restaurant visit, serious foodies go on fact-finding missions online to research their meals in advance.

The problem is that entering a restaurant with so many preconceived notions removes the spontaneity from the experience. You might end up missing a nugget of culinary history about Lobster Newburg from the waiter (who would tell you the dish originated at Delmonico's Restaurant in New York City in 1876 from a recipe credited to a frequent guest of the restaurant, Ben Wenberg, that was later refined by Chef

Charles Ranhofer) or a primer on the nuances of Creole- versus Cajun-style gumbo (Creole-style is commonly made with okra, tomato, and a combination of meat and seafood, while the Cajun version is spicier, typically tomato free, and thickened with a dark roux).

It may feel like flying without a parachute, but I think it's always best to enter a restaurant knowing as little about the menu as possible. Do you read ten different film reviews before every movie you see? Probably not. Of course, it's always nice to know when critics recommend a film, but in my opinion, film criticism is often more illuminating to read *after* you see the movie and have formulated your own opinions about it. Researching restaurants in advance creates unnecessary biases and inflates expectations in a way that can adversely affect your dining experiences.

AVOID "STORYBOARDING" YOUR MEALS

Having unfettered access to troves of online data from sites like Yelp and Tripadvisor leads many people to do what I call "storyboarding" their restaurant meals. *Storyboarding* is a term that film directors use for planning out the composition of every shot in a movie by drawing individual slides of each scene beforehand. When diners storyboard their restaurant experiences, they meticulously plan out their menu to the exact dish, often refusing to even consider items that weren't enthusiastically recommended by others online.

Assuming you or your guests don't have serious dietary restrictions that require game planning in advance, you should always try to enter a restaurant without a prescribed plan. Restaurant menus change frequently, especially those that are dictated by seasonal ingredients such as heirloom tomatoes, morel mushrooms, or soft-shell crabs. A friend might tell you, "You have to try the crispy duck with satsumas!"—one of the chef's specialties. But your friend may also never have tried the spot prawns with fairytale eggplant and Thai green curry because it wasn't on the menu when they visited in the winter months. If you simply order the duck without even considering the rest of the menu, you may be cheating yourself out of unexpected surprises.

THE MYTH OF THE SIGNATURE DISH

To most professional chefs, a signature dish does not exist. The term likely began as a food media fabrication that entered the lexicon with the rise of celebrity chefs in the late 1990s and into the early 2000s, when restaurants exploded in popularity. Suddenly, chefs needed a calling card, and restaurants centered their marketing schemes around certain "can't-miss" dishes such as yellowfin tuna sashimi with ponzu or molten chocolate lava cake with Madagascar vanilla ice cream that helped them stand out from the crowd.

Over time, signature recipes became like hit pop songs. Once certain chefs broke through with a big hit, they played it over and over to delighted crowds. Thomas Keller became known for the salmon tartare cornets (miniature black sesame tuiles shaped like ice cream cones filled with minced raw salmon and red onion crème fraîche) that he originally served at the French Laundry in Napa Valley; Nobu Matsuhisa burst onto the culinary scene with his miso-marinated black cod at Nobu in New York City; and Alice Waters thumbed her nose at the food cognoscenti by serving a simple Frog Hollow Farm peach on a plate at Chez Panisse in Berkeley. Even chain restaurants have their own signature dishes—like the Bourbon Street Chicken and Shrimp at Applebee's or the Bloomin' Onion at Outback Steakhouse. As restaurants became status symbols, diners embraced the idea that every restaurant or chef has one standout dish that towers above the rest. But in most cases, that simply isn't true.

People who work in restaurants know that signature dishes aren't always the best items on the menu. But it can be difficult at times to convince guests to stray from the herd. Chefs, who put hours of work into creating a menu with a breadth of options, can become frustrated when a majority of customers order the exact same thing. I once worked with a pastry chef who would regularly remove one of her most popular desserts, a maple mascarpone cheesecake, from the menu because she was so tired of selling thirty of them every night while her latest creation, which she labored over for days, went virtually unsold.

Chefs are constantly finding new inspiration in unfamiliar ingredients, techniques, and recipes. Only ordering whatever menu items are

considered signatures is like only playing the greatest hits of your favorite artist. There's nothing wrong with listening to the tried-and-true
chart-toppers, but your love of an artist's most popular songs shouldn't
stop you from sampling their latest album either.

FOOD CRITICS DON'T KNOW EVERYTHING

I can't tell you how many times I've clicked on a food critic's scathing
review about a restaurant that I personally enjoyed. Taste in food is very
subjective, and a food writer's opinion should never be taken as gospel.
But when big-name restaurant critics weigh in on new restaurants, their
reviews are highly influential, the same way that the Michelin Guide is
followed religiously across the globe. I saw the effect firsthand in high-
profile restaurants that were reviewed while I was still working there.
After the reviews came out, whatever dishes the critic praised immediately became top sellers. I always found it somewhat surprising that so
many people put so much faith in one person's opinion.

Of course, many of these guests would also leave disappointed because they had prioritized a critic's opinion over their own personal
taste. Rather than share the negative feedback about the dish with the
server, some of them take to social media after the fact to excoriate the
food and slander the critic. "I don't know why Pete Wells [the former
New York Times restaurant critic] thinks that the venison is so special,"
they proclaim. "Mine was dry and flavorless, but I guess it tastes better
when the *New York Times* is paying for it."

You should never order only whatever others say is good at a restaurant. You should order the dishes that best suit *you* and your personal
taste. Sometimes following your inner voice will lead you astray, but
trusting your instincts means that your own preferences are centered,
not some random tastemaker's or food writer's. Think about restaurant
experiences like going to the movies. Have you ever seen a film that a
friend enthusiastically recommended, but that you thought was trash?
Our taste in food is as subjective as it is in film, art, and music. It's rare
to find consensus about great songs or paintings. It's the same with

restaurant food. That's why it's better to listen to you own inner voice about what to order, instead of slavishly following the "experts."

USE YOUR SERVER AS A GUIDE, NOT AN AUTHORITY

When I worked at the Hong Kong location of the famous New York red sauce joint, I was surprised how rarely guests would ask me, a genuine New Yorker who had traveled thousands of miles to work there, for recommendations on the menu. On a nightly basis, guests would shoo me away whenever I approached the table to offer help with their choices. I'd even catch some of them googling photos of the food or reading online reviews while I was standing right there. Perhaps it was intimidating for some locals who weren't familiar with Italian American dishes like clams oreganata or chicken scarpariello, but I can't help thinking that many guests would have enjoyed their meal more if they had taken a moment to chat with me about the food.

Even though the restaurant was halfway around the world from the original, guests in Hong Kong fired off Number Ones at a heavy clip— Caesar salad, spicy rigatoni with meatballs, and veal parmesan—exactly like everyone did at the flagship back in New York City. It turns out our clientele overseas approached their dining experiences similarly to their American counterparts; they also wanted to feel like they were enjoying the restaurant's finest dishes. But they were also missing out on some of the most delicious (albeit less heralded) menu items—charred octopus with cherry peppers, beef carpaccio with black truffle, and veal chop marsala with porcini mushroom, among others.

Trusting your instincts is important, but you should always engage with your server before you order food in any restaurant, even when you're struggling to decide on a sandwich at a takeout counter. Talk to the people who work there. Instead of asking them about their favorite dishes, use them as a resource to direct you to menu items that suit your preferences. When I was a waiter, people would always ask me, "What's your favorite thing on the menu?" When I answered, "I love the roasted

Sharing Is Caring

Not every guest is comfortable sharing, but ordering dishes for the table instead of individually can be an effective strategy for everyone in your party to taste a wider variety of food. Some menus—like the ones you find in trendy small-plate restaurants—are already designed to be shared, but even those that aren't can usually be enjoyed when you approach them with a team concept. If you prefer to share family style, always consult with your server beforehand to find the menus items that are best suited for sharing. Experienced servers might dissuade you from ordering a bouillabaisse [French-style seafood stew], for example, because they know that divvying up hot broth among four people is awkward and frustrating. Although it doesn't hurt to ask, never expect a restaurant to divide individual dishes for you in the kitchen when you're sharing. Many chefs still refuse to split food on separate plates because it compromises the intended presentation. This is why building strong relationships with staff is so important and how it can lead to more accommodating service. If you have a good rapport with your server, they're more likely to be a persistent advocate for your needs in the kitchen.

chicken!" they'd look disappointed and mumble something like, "Sorry, I don't really like chicken." These interactions happen all the time in restaurants because asking servers what *they* like is the wrong question.

A more productive approach is to ask your server targeted questions with specific prompts that more directly reflect your preferences. If you're a seafood lover, for example, you might tell the server: "I think I'm in the mood for seafood tonight. Would you recommend the wood-grilled striped bass or the dover sole meunière?" Offering parameters helps focus the conversation. Framing menu questions with details about your dietary preferences is also an effective way to get more targeted recommendations. Preface your question like this: "I don't love dishes that are cooked with too much butter or cream, can you recommend an appetizer that's on the lighter side?" or "The last time I was here I had the cavatelli pasta with pesto and shrimp, which was delicious. What other pasta would you recommend?"

Framing these menu questions with your personal preferences helps servers provide more educated responses. Soliciting a drink recommendation by saying, "I love dirty martinis and strong bitter drinks—which one of your featured cocktails would you recommend?" is much more effective than asking, "What's your favorite cocktail on the menu?" In the former scenario, the server should offer a recommendation of something stirred and spirit forward, tailored to your guidance. In the latter, they're more likely to default to suggestions based on their own personal preferences or popularity.

A caveat here: relying on a server's expertise comes with some degree of risk because not all front-of-house staff are equally competent at their jobs. So tread lightly when you encounter a server who lacks polish or seems inexperienced.

THERE IS MORE THAN ONE PATH
TO A SUCCESSFUL MEAL

One of the things I found most tragic about the popularity of the Number One was how often guests seemed underwhelmed by it. As a server, I always felt powerless because these guests hadn't given me an opportunity to help them consider better options. Sadly, we live in a world driven by FOMO (fear of missing out), and that fear can be especially strong in restaurants. Whenever people see a line outside the latest hotspot, the forbidden fruit makes them obsess even more about getting a reservation.

If having the "best" meal at a restaurant means ordering one specific dish over another, then it probably isn't a great restaurant. Unfortunately, too many guests approach restaurant visits with the mentality that they have to stick to the signature dishes they've heard and read about to maximize their experience. It's a strategy that regularly backfires. On top of that, menus change frequently, so going in with tunnel vision makes it easy to miss out on dishes that are only available for a limited time, such as buttery Nantucket Bay scallops, succulent Dungeness crab, or a perfectly ripe persimmon.

It's always best to approach dining out with an open mind. Never assume that skipping the most famous dishes on the menu means that you're cheating yourself out of having a great experience. Truthfully, you end up cheating yourself more by limiting your choices to the most popular items. There is no such thing as an "ideal order" in any restaurant, at least not one that will appeal to every guest. Have faith that whatever path you choose will lead to the best experience for you personally.

THE TAKEAWAY

Restaurant visits shouldn't be scripted. It's easy to fall prey to the idea that researching a restaurant in advance and plotting out your menu choices beforehand is essential to preparedness. But doing so detracts from the spontaneity. Signature dishes, though they may be the best reviewed or most talked about items, don't always suit every guest's taste. Treat every dining experience like a blank slate and try to consult with the staff before planning every meal. Following the herd might be the safest path, but it can often lead you astray.

CHAPTER FIVE

How to Ask the Right Questions

One time I went into a restaurant, and I asked
the waiter for some food for thought. He left, came back,
and tried shoving a sirloin in my ear.

—TRAVIS JEREMIAH DAHNKE

The language you use in a restaurant is critical to getting what you want. Unfortunately, many diners lack the vocabulary to properly ask for things. The key to communicating your needs effectively is to present special requests using language that acknowledges the complexity of what you're asking. Guests will often present their requests too casually or in a way that implies that whatever they're asking for is easy, which, in a restaurant, it never is. Servers may be less inclined to help when you present complicated requests—like veganizing a dish that isn't vegan—as simple tasks.

A good habit to get into is to preface your special requests with "whenever you have a chance" or "there's no rush" to signal to your server that you appreciate the effort involved in accommodating something out of the ordinary. Servers have the unenviable task of chaperoning hundreds of strangers through their meals every week, having to navigate their eccentricities while also making sure that every detail of their dining experience is perfect. Imagine how difficult it must be to do that night after night without incident. Most of us can't cook a meal for our own families at home and make everyone happy.

Try not to preface requests by saying, "They've done this for me before," even if the restaurant *has* done something for you before. Nothing that happened in a restaurant yesterday matters today. It's possible that the kitchen wasn't as busy during your previous visit, so the chef might have been more willing to make you something special off the menu. Saying "They've done this for me before" implies that being unable to accommodate the request again would be inhospitable. But extenuating factors change. This is why chefs often have such rigid rules about allowing guests to make substitutions or customize their menu. Chefs know that accommodating every exotic request sets a dangerous precedent that can't be consistently replicated. In my experience, entitled guests are often willing to embellish their accounts about the nature of past accommodations because they think it makes it harder for the staff to say no. But when a staff is well-versed on the house rules, these embellishments usually backfire at the expense of the server-guest relationship.

Keep in mind that there isn't necessarily a right or wrong way to ask for something in a restaurant, but there are certainly better or worse approaches. Here are some common scenarios with helpful strategies on how to engage the staff.

WHEN YOU NEED HELP GETTING A TABLE

Everyone asks the same question when a restaurant is impossible to get into: *Who do I need to know to get a reservation at this place?* Beyond having a personal connection with the owner or a friend who works there, there probably isn't a secret code or a private unlisted number to get you in. Most of the time, it comes down to supply and demand. When demand for tables outstrips supply, seating becomes scarcer. It's that simple. Everyone also wants an 8:00 p.m. reservation, so prime-time slots are often booked out even further in advance.

Most restaurants have limited space for larger parties. When a party is six or more people, for example, the restaurant may only have a few tables that can accommodate parties of that size, which can make the reservation process even more challenging. If you're serious about dining somewhere, it's important to be flexible with reservation times and be willing to accept a time slot that might be less than ideal.

If you have difficulty procuring a suitable reservation time online, it doesn't hurt to pick up the phone or show up to the restaurant in person if you live nearby. A real human being might be more sympathetic to your predicament. But spare the staff your sob story about how you've been *dying* to eat there or the guilt trip over how hard it is to get a table. They've heard it all before. Chances are, you're not going to get exactly what you want, but the person on the other end of the line might have some valuable insights or strategies for making reservations in the future.

It always helps to frame your reservation request in a positive light. Tell the reservationist: "I've heard so much about your restaurant, but I haven't had any luck making a reservation online. Do you have any suggestions on how to increase my chances of getting a table?" The reservationist may have some helpful insights like Tuesdays are the easiest night to get in or calling the restaurant in the afternoon to check for cancellations that day can often result in scoring a last-minute table.

If you walk into any restaurant without a reservation, be willing to return the table quickly. Even the shrewdest gatekeepers are far more likely to accommodate guests who are willing to agree to a scheduled out-by time. Rather than walking in and simply asking, "Do you have anything available now for a party of two?" use more collaborative language like "Is there any chance you could seat two of us for a quick dinner? We promise to have the table back quickly." Maître d's and hosts are always more open to doing favors for people who are willing to reciprocate.

WHEN YOU NEED A COCKTAIL OR WINE RECOMMENDATION

Guests often ask overly vague questions when they need help choosing wine or cocktails. For example, people will ask the server: "Could you recommend a dry white wine?" It's a perfectly reasonable question, but it leaves a lot open for interpretation. Everyone's idea of dryness in wine is much different. A more effective strategy would be to offer your server a specific frame of reference for what you *do* like. Prefacing your question with a few examples—"I typically like a Sancerre or pinot grigio"—gives the server a clearer idea about what type of wine you like aside from its dryness.

Choosing wine can be intimidating. If you don't feel like you have the proper vocabulary to ask for help, be upfront and honest about that. Admitting the limitations of your wine and spirits knowledge is a sign of strength. It also helps the person serving you more accurately gauge your level of expertise. It's much harder for a server to help someone who pretends to know about wine than someone who can admit they don't. There is no need to denigrate yourself. Guests too often make self-deprecating comments when they aren't wine savvy like "I'm not a connoisseur" or "I don't have a very educated palate." You should never apologize for your inexperience. Instead, demonstrate an interest in learning and an adventurous spirit.

If you have any trepidation about the server's recommendation for a wine by the glass, kindly ask if you can have a small taste before committing to it. Some servers will automatically offer a taste first before pouring a full glass anyway to avoid wasting product, but it's always wise to ask just in case. If you're torn between two different wines, politely ask the server if they'd be willing to let you try both. But never treat this process like you're asking for a private wine tasting, which can damage your relationship with the server.

If you need help navigating the bottled wine list, it's helpful to offer price parameters. Asking a server or sommelier to recommend a "full-bodied Italian red" isn't as effective as saying: "Can you recommend an Italian red between eighty and a hundred dollars? I tend to like old-world wines that are more peppery or earthy." Even though talking about price can be uncomfortable in certain situations, being candid about your wine budget helps the staff avoid offending you by recommending a bottle that's out of your price range.

Cocktail culture has also exploded in recent years, which can make conversations at the bar more intimidating. Staying informed and keeping up with bar trends and newfangled techniques isn't easy for casual drinkers. In a tiki bar, for example, a single drink might have eight or ten different components; the average drinker might only be able to identify half of them. It's fine to ask the bartender to explain the unfamiliar ingredients, but that doesn't always help you understand what the cocktail tastes like.

Instead, ask the bartender to compare the cocktail that interests you to another more commonly known drink. There may not be a perfect analogy, but it will keep the conversation focused on how the drink tastes instead of the unfamiliar ingredients that go into it. Rather than interrogating the bartender with specific questions like "What is Amaro Nonino?" or "Can you explain pineapple gum syrup?" a more productive approach would be to ask: "How do you prepare this scotch-based cocktail? Is it stirred like a Rob Roy?" or "Do you think the rum cocktail with black walnut bitters would be a good choice if I like to drink old-fashioneds?"

WHEN YOU NEED ASSISTANCE WITH THE MENU

Every waiter's pet peeve is when guests ask, "What's good here?" It's a perfectly reasonable question to ask, but it's also a very lazy one. Would you walk into a car dealership and ask the salesperson, "What's a good car?" Of course not. You would say, "I'm looking for an SUV that seats up to five people, with decent gas mileage, four-wheel drive, and a sunroof. I don't want to spend more than sixty thousand dollars." If you want someone in a restaurant to help you choose dishes that best suit your preferences, it helps to communicate what those preferences are.

The reason that servers hate the dreaded "What's good here?" question is because generic questions invite generic answers. Most of the time, servers are too busy to present every table with an exhaustive list of their favorite menu items. If they do have time, great. But if they don't, it makes life easier when guests narrow the scope of their questions to the dishes that suit their own personal taste.

Be as specific as possible when you ask about the menu. Targeted questions will invite more vivid descriptions rather than simply soliciting the waiter's opinion about whether they like a dish or not. For example, you might ask: "I was thinking about ordering the sockeye salmon. Can you tell me more about the lemon caper dill sauce?" To keep the discussion focused on your personal preferences, just like when you're soliciting wine help, present the waiter with choices that appeal to you and ask which one they recommend. Instead of asking about the best dessert, for instance, you could say, "I'd love to try one of your desserts—which do you prefer between the raspberry millefeuille and the matcha crème brûlée?"

It's best to avoid framing questions in a way that puts your server on the spot, even when you present them playfully. You might find it amusing to raise the stakes by asking, "If you could only eat here one time and you could order anything on the menu, what would it be?" but your server might not be in the mood for role-playing. It may seem like these "stranded on a deserted island" scenarios are a fun way to spark up a conversation about the menu, but you'll always get more direct answers when you keep your questions direct and the hypotheticals to a minimum.

Contrary to what many guests believe, it doesn't hurt servers' feelings when people don't take their recommendations. But if a server goes out of their way to make specific suggestions on the menu and you don't take their advice, at least acknowledge that you appreciate their input. Before you order alternatives, you might say something like, "Everything you recommended sounds *amazing*, but I think I'm more in the mood to have the grilled mahi-mahi tonight." If you don't acknowledge the effort, servers may feel like you were just wasting their time.

WHEN YOU'D LIKE TO MOVE
TO A DIFFERENT TABLE

Everyone wants to sit at the best table in the restaurant. Unfortunately, not everyone can have the cozy corner banquette. Most restaurants also have less desirable tables that everyone hates, the ones that are situated too close to the bathrooms or in highly congested areas. If you decide to ask for a different table, it's always best to include a reason why you'd like to move. It won't guarantee that management will accommodate you, but it will make you seem like less of a diva for wanting to relocate. If someone in your party is very tall, for example, explain to the host or maître d' that a table with additional legroom would be more comfortable for them.

Keep in mind that different tables in the dining room are meant to accommodate different party sizes. If you're a party of three that wants to move, you shouldn't point to a large booth that's set for six people and ask to be seated there instead. When a table is open, it doesn't always mean the table is available. In most cases, the maître d' has a future plan to seat it. Most busy restaurants plot their reservations very carefully with little room for error, so accommodating everyone's preferred seating arrangement can be difficult. If you're dissatisfied with your table when you sit down, you should communicate your displeasure as quickly as possible. It's much harder for a restaurant to change your table in the middle of your meal.

If you don't plan to occupy the table very long, let the host know that when you ask to move. You might say something like, "Would it be possible to have a larger banquette table? We're feeling a little cramped here. We can promise to have the table back by 8:15 p.m." The maître d' may be more willing to take a chance on giving away a larger table (or a more desirable one) if they know they'll have the table turned quickly for a larger party or VIP guests that are arriving later. If you've agreed to return the table, do not renege on your end of the bargain when it's time to leave. Maître d's have extremely stressful and difficult jobs. Burn them once and you may never get another reservation again.

WHEN YOU THINK
THE MUSIC IS TOO LOUD

I worked for over ten years at a downtown New York City restaurant that was notorious for playing loud rock music. It was a point of pride for the chef-owner, who reveled in the dichotomy of delivering elegant food and service against the backdrop of blaring AC/DC on the stereo system. I think part of the allure for him was challenging people's expectations of what fine dining is supposed to be, but he also really wanted to create a party-like atmosphere where guests felt like they were having a good time. Of course, many guests would arrive with certain expectations about the atmosphere that would be instantly shattered by the volume and genre of the music. But we almost never turned the volume down when guests complained.

I hate to say it, but when you dine out in someone else's restaurant, you don't get to choose the soundtrack or decide what the ambience is like. Whether you like it or not, it's up to the owners to decide how much to dim the lighting and how loud the stereo should be played. Music is very divisive; no playlist will make everyone in the dining room happy. One guest might be charmed by the nostalgia of a mellow Frank Sinatra song, while another guest might find the choice stuffy and languid.

If you think the music is too loud, there are ways to communicate that it's bothering you without getting upset. First, never complain that you can't hear the conversation at the table. A restaurant is not a library or a quiet car on a train. It's supposed to be a festive environment for everyone, and there are many guests who prefer to dine in a lively atmosphere with upbeat music. It's fine if you aren't a Prince fan, but that doesn't mean you have a right to tell a restaurant not to play "Purple Rain" in its entirety.

The best strategy when asking for the music to be turned down (or changed to a softer genre) is to first acknowledge that you understand that the music is part of the vibe. Politely convey to your server that you aren't feeling it. In this case, a self-deprecating approach can be effective. You might say something like, "I'm sorry, I don't want to kill the vibe, but would it be possible to turn the music down a smidge?" Inquiring about the possibility of lowering the volume rather than making a demand to turn it down is key. If management decides not to adjust the volume or change the music to mollify you, it's imperative to respect their choice. When you dine in a restaurant, you are a guest, and every guest can't be the deejay.

WHEN YOU HAVE
SPECIAL DIETARY NEEDS

It's always best to make a note about your food allergies or dietary preferences when you first make a reservation. Keep your messaging succinct and avoid exaggeration or embellishment. Extraneous language could result in the restaurant missing pertinent information about your dietary needs. Lines of communication can easily get crossed in a busy restaurant, so even if you've noted an allergy on your reservation, it's important to remind the server about it when you discuss the menu, so they can provide suggestions about which dishes are or aren't safe for you to eat. This way the information about your dietary restrictions is fresh in their mind when they place your order.

While restaurants should always do their best to accommodate guests with serious food allergies, they won't always be able to invent dishes that are specifically tailored to every individual's needs. Never frame a special request in a way that makes you seem entitled because of your dietary restraints. For example, saying to the waiter, "I'm deathly allergic to alliums—can the chef prepare the branzino for me but simply steamed with olive oil, lemon, and maybe some fresh herbs?" is not as productive as asking, "For someone who can't have alliums, is it possible to make the branzino without any garlic or onions?" Restaurants take food allergies more and more seriously these days. As a result, staff have become more adept at offering guidance to guests with allergies and more educated about the dangers associated with them.

Don't forget: *your server is a mouthpiece for your needs in the kitchen.* So it's best to keep them squarely in your corner. When you have a real dietary concern or food allergy, it's always wise to defer to the staff's expertise. Solicit the server's recommendations by asking specific questions that highlight the dietary issue like, "Which is the best pasta dish that doesn't have any shellfish? I'm severely allergic." As much as possible, try to stay within the framework of the menu to find suitable options, instead of making demands about bespoke items. As long as you don't sound entitled, it's fine to ask for minor modifications. You might say: "Would it be possible to have the fajitas made without any cilantro? I'm very allergic to it."

When I was waiting tables, I always appreciated when guests were specific about the nature of their allergic reactions. I think it makes the danger more real for servers when a guest says something like, "If I go anywhere near a pistachio, my face will blow up like a balloon." Not everyone is comfortable sharing granular details about their allergic reactions, but if an ingredient causes anaphylaxis, for example, it's critical for the server to understand that the reaction is more severe than someone simply breaking out in hives.

Is It a Dietary Restriction or Food Allergy?

It can be very frustrating for servers when guests conflate their dietary restrictions with more serious, life-threatening food allergies. Technically speaking, food allergies, which can be deadly, are caused by the body's immune system producing a physiological response to proteins found in certain foods. A dietary restriction or food intolerance is far less severe and involves the need to reduce or limit specific foods from one's diet. When a guest has a food allergy, the server will typically alert the chef to the nature and severity of the issue. Most restaurants also train staff to attach notes about a guest's specific allergens when they place the order. Dietary preferences aren't typically treated with the same gravitas. It's become more common practice in restaurants for servers to preemptively ask about food allergies and dietary restrictions. You should never exaggerate the severity of a dietary preference. When guests refer to their new keto diet as though they're deathly allergic to carbs, it creates unnecessary noise that makes it harder for patrons with serious allergies to have their voices heard. Chefs are simply too busy to treat every situation in which garlic upsets someone's stomach as cause for sterilizing every utensil in the kitchen.

WHEN YOU WANT SEPARATE CHECKS

When guests want separate itemized checks, they often inform the server right away. In my opinion, it's much better to wait until the end of the meal to discuss how you'd like to split payment. Making demands about separate checks when you first sit down can negatively affect your first impression. I understand that some diners are on a strict budget, like elderly guests or businesspeople traveling on expense accounts, but itemizing the bill isn't nearly as easy as most guests think. In fact, it can be a very time-consuming and tedious process, especially for waiters who have a million other things to do.

Most restaurant point-of-sale software has some functionality that allows servers to itemize checks, but it usually requires that these items be separated manually, one at a time. If you are a party of six asking for split checks, for example, it could take your waiter up to ten minutes to go back and figure out what each person ordered and then separate those items onto six individual tabs. If anything was shared for the table, like bottled water or communal appetizers, the software systems might not be able to divide the cost of those items evenly across multiple checks, which complicates the calculus of splitting the bill even more.

If you're paying with multiple credit cards, the easiest way to handle split payment is to ask the server to divide the bill into separate monetary amounts. Ideally, you'd find a way to split the check evenly among your tablemates, to simplify the process for the server. If the division is more complicated, write down the dollar amounts you'd like your server to charge each credit card with the corresponding name or numbers on the card. Acknowledge that it's an inconvenience by saying: "We're sorry to make this so complicated, but we'd like to divide the bill on four different cards. Could you please charge each card with the amounts we wrote down for you?" If you do split payment on multiple cards, make sure that your calculations don't end up shortchanging the server's gratuity. This happens often when whoever is in charge of calculating each person's share doesn't properly communicate how much everyone should be tipping on their portion of the bill.

THE TAKEAWAY

Language is so important in how you communicate your needs in a restaurant. Use it to your advantage. How you phrase a question can often be the difference between getting what you want or putting off a member of the staff. Nothing you ask for in a restaurant is ever easy, so make sure to present special requests in a way that acknowledges the effort it will take to accommodate them.

CHAPTER SIX

Learning to Decode Waiter-Speak

The best number for a dinner party is two:
myself and a damn good head waiter.

—NUBAR GULBENKIAN

As a young server in the late 1990s, I once witnessed a chef berating a fellow server after overhearing him tell guests that he preferred one dish on the menu over another. "We don't pay you to have opinions!" the chef bellowed, after summoning him back into the kitchen like a parent reprimanding their child. I certainly don't condone the chef's abusive approach, but looking back, his argument has merit. Great servers should act as guides, not food critics, and while I think many guests appreciate the candor, a waiter's unadulterated opinions can be easily misconstrued as disrespectful toward the kitchen's work.

There's a fine art to "waiter-speak," the coded vernacular servers use to stay in everyone's good graces. Waiter-speak can help servers conceal blind spots in their menu knowledge or evade blame when a guest is unhappy with their food. To survive as a server, you have to be a constant buffer between the guest's needs and the chef's ego. These forces are often diametrically opposed, with the server stuck in the middle, like when a guest sends back a steak that's cooked perfectly. A nimble server will insist the guest is crazy when they bring the food back to the chef, then turn around and offer the chef's sincerest apologies to the guest for the problems with their food (even though the entire kitchen staff likely spent the last five minutes slandering them).

The best waiters are skilled diplomats. When making menu suggestions, they know how to make guests feel like they arrived at their decisions on their own, knowing full well that they might be held responsible if any items they recommended turn out to be disappointing. Waiter-speak often saves guests from making bad decisions. Once, someone asked me if I recommended the sweetbreads on the menu. When I was growing up, my Argentinian-born father used to grill sweetbreads (thymus glands, typically from a calf) and serve them with chimichurri sauce. But I could sense that this guest seemed a little apprehensive, so I prefaced my recommendation with a caveat: "As long as you're a fan of organ meats, the sweetbreads are wonderful." Once she learned that sweetbreads were offal and not some kind of "sweet bread" the chef made, she ordered something else. My waiter-speak rescued her from the disappointment, and embarrassment, of ordering something she likely wouldn't have enjoyed and possibly may have found disgusting.

Even at the world's finest restaurants, waiters often haven't tasted every dish on the menu. Food costs are way too high for chefs to fire up a two-hundred-dollar Wagyu steak just so every member of the staff can accurately describe it to guests. New trainees are often thrown into the fire with only a packet of printed menu descriptions and a few days of training under their belts, forced to rely on instincts to feign competency. Without firsthand experience tasting certain food items, many servers rely on waiter-speak out of necessity to sound more knowledgeable than they really are.

If they want to stay gainfully employed, servers must also learn to censor themselves when guests ask mundane questions or behave rudely. Veiled language can be a clever way to hide disdain or to avoid confrontation. Once you're able to recognize the hidden meaning behind the waiter-speak, it's much easier to understand what your server really means.

Here's an interaction between a waiter and a guest discussing the evening's specials that you will *never* hear in a restaurant:

GUEST: How's the special red snapper?

WAITER: Honestly, we've been running it as a featured item for the past few days, and it hasn't really been selling too well. It might not be that fresh, so I'd probably order the steak au poivre or herb-roasted chicken instead.

In reality, the interaction will likely sound more like this:

GUEST: How's the special red snapper?

WAITER: The fish is very popular tonight! You can't go wrong with the specials, but I think I'm a little partial to the classics on our menu like the steak au poivre or the herb-roasted chicken.

The waiter's message in both examples is essentially the same: don't order the special red snapper. But the obvious difference is how the waiter sugarcoats the answer in the second example to portray the special in a more positive light while also gently redirecting the guest toward other options on the menu. A trained ear will be able to recognize these moments when they happen, to better discern what a server is really saying. Decoding the message can help save you from making bad choices, overstaying your welcome, or even offending the staff.

Not every waiter communicates the same. Some are more candid about their opinions. Others play it closer to the vest. But always keep in mind that what a waiter says and what they mean can often be two entirely different things. You should never automatically take what the waiter says at face value. Here are some common examples of waiter-speak with accompanying translations:

WAITER SAYS: "Have you dined with us before?"

TRANSLATION: I'll spare you the menu spiel if you're already familiar with it.

This question has become so ubiquitous in restaurants that it's almost laughable to hear at this point. Sometimes the phrase comes across as condescending, especially to experienced diners who feel perfectly capable of navigating a menu without any hand-holding. But when servers ask this question, it's meant to determine a table's familiarity the menu and to identify repeat guests. This helps them establish the degree to which they'll need to explain the menu format and offer recommendations. At many restaurants, from fining dining to casual chains, servers are trained to deliver a "spiel" to every table with an overview of the rules of engagement. When guests have never dined in a particular restaurant before, these precursory remarks can provide important context, especially in places that serve family-style portions meant for sharing or in tapas-style restaurants with small plates. Without a proper menu spiel, first-timers will likely end up ordering too much or too little food.

WAITER SAYS: "That's one of our biggest sellers by far!"

TRANSLATION: It's popular but not necessarily my favorite.

Skilled waiters know that the most popular dishes on the menu aren't always the best. It isn't true in every case, of course, but sometimes when servers tell you that a dish is popular, they're hiding the fact that they think it's a case of style over substance. If a server tells you, "People love it!" or "We always sell out of that dish," it doesn't always mean the same as "It's one of my top choices!" or "I always recommend it." Waiters are human databases. They're in the trenches every day, gathering feedback from customer responses and storing the information to better serve new customers. If you ask the right questions and listen carefully to the answers, the waiter will steer you toward quality not popularity.

WAITER SAYS: "I would recommend it, as long as you like spicy flavors."

TRANSLATION: People complain that the dish is too spicy all the time.

When your server issues caveats like this, it can often be intended as a warning or disclaimer. Calling attention to controversial flavor profiles like sweet, salty, or spicy can often signal that some guests find the flavors in a particular dish off-putting or overpowering. If you love spicy food, then you have nothing to worry about. But if you're sensitive to it, it might make sense to order something else when a server makes a comment like this. Avoid asking servers to adjust the spice level of a dish to your taste. Perfectly calibrating the amount of spice to suit everyone's unique palate is impossible, especially given the subjective nature of what spicy means to different people. No chef wants to waste food because a dish that was ordered less spicy ends up being too spicy for the guest who ordered it. Pro tip: ask the server if the kitchen can bring the spicy component (like chili flakes or fresh jalapeños) on the side, so you can adjust the spice level to your taste.

> **WAITER SAYS:** "It's so hard to compare—those are two of my favorite dishes. I love them both equally."
>
> **TRANSLATION:** You're probably going to blame me if I choose one over the other and you don't like my choice, so I'd rather not commit.

Waitstaff love offering guidance, but when guests corner us to recommend one dish over the other, they often hold us responsible if the results disappoint. Whenever it feels like a guest is setting a trap, experienced waiters will shift into neutral and assume a more diplomatic stance. They'll highlight the relative strengths of each dish and leave it to the guest to decide. If the waiter does recommend one dish over the other, there's at least a 50 percent chance the guest won't like it and a 100 percent chance that if they don't, they'll make a passive-aggressive comment about how they should try the other dish next time.

> **WAITER SAYS:** "It's a perfect wine if you're looking for something dry and medium-bodied."
>
> **TRANSLATION:** I've never tasted the wine before.

Within the category of waiter-speak, there is a subcategory I call "wine-speak." The best restaurants rigorously train their staff to be fluent on the wine list, but it takes time and money to get a team with varying degrees of oenological aptitude up to speed. If a restaurant has hundreds of selections on its wine list, there's a pretty good chance that most servers have tasted only a small fraction of them. Some upscale restaurants have the budget to hire a sommelier who can provide more comprehensive support on the floor, but most mid-tier restaurants rely on their waitstaff and managers to help guests choose wine. You can often gauge the level of expertise a staff member has by how vague or specific their answers are to wine-related inquiries. If you ask about a specific bottle and the server describes it using broad terms like *fruity* or *oaky*, there's a good chance they're unfamiliar with the wine you're asking about.

WAITER SAYS: "Can I bring you something to start?"

TRANSLATION: If you don't order any appetizers, you're going to be waiting a long time for your main courses to arrive.

Most diners think when waiters are pushy about selling appetizers that it's simply a ploy to boost the check. Not always. Aside from wanting their tables to spend more, servers also know that the kitchen can be burdened by what we call "order fire" tickets. An order fire ticket is a one-course order consisting only of main courses. When the kitchen gets too many order fire tickets, it puts undue strain on parts of the line, such as the grill station, where main course proteins like meats and fish are cooked. An appetizer course provides a buffer that allows the expediter more leeway to stagger the timing of firing each table's mains. An order fire ticket, because the food needs to be prepared right away, jumps ahead in the line, which means that tables that have already had appetizers and are waiting for their main courses will likely be delayed. If you aren't that hungry, simply decline the offer, but you shouldn't assume that the server is trying to strong-arm you into ordering more food.

WAITER SAYS: "Let me check with the chef to see if we can do that."

TRANSLATION: The chef is almost certainly going to say no, but I want you to think I'm doing my best to accommodate your request.

Any food-related modifications or special requests must be approved by the chef. Servers often conveniently rely on the "idea" of the chef as a scapegoat when they have to say no. In many cases, a server has already asked the chef the same question in the recent past, so they already know the answer. If the chef said no the last time, it's highly unlikely they'll suddenly have a change of heart. But most customers would not respond positively to a server saying, "I asked the chef the same question last week, and they told me they couldn't do it." So waiters often promise to ask the chef, anyway, to keep up the appearance that they're trying, even though they know that a negative outcome is a foregone conclusion. On some occasions, like when the chef is in a bad mood, servers won't even bother asking. They'll disappear into the kitchen for a minute or two, then reappear with the predetermined bad news, without having exchanged a word with the chef. In some restaurants, these little white lies keep us alive to fight another day.

WAITER SAYS: "Sorry, there was a miscommunication in the kitchen about your order."

TRANSLATION: I totally screwed everything up, but I'm hoping if I say it's the kitchen's fault that you won't be upset with me.

Even the most honest waiters occasionally throw the kitchen under the bus. We're not proud when we need to cover up our mistakes by scapegoating the kitchen, but doing so can be a convenient crutch when things go awry. Guests aren't always charitable about forgiving human error, so waiters can be hesitant to come clean when they've made a mistake. They may also be reluctant to admit fault to avoid putting their tips in jeopardy. Of course, miscommunication in the kitchen happens all the time, so it's possible the server might be telling the truth. But when waiters are quick to blame the kitchen for a mistake, they're almost always trying to cover their tracks. Don't feel too much sympathy for the kitchen staff either. They throw servers under the bus all the time too.

WAITER SAYS: "I apologize for the delay on your food. It should be here any minute."

TRANSACTION: I'm praying it arrives soon, but I'm too scared to ask the chef about it.

When a table's food is dragging, servers know it helps to visit the table to acknowledge the delay and reassure them that their food is on the way. But when the kitchen gets slammed, waiters aren't always privy to actionable intelligence about how soon the food will arrive. In the heat of battle, the chef is also more focused on getting food out as quickly as possible rather than wasting energy quoting ticket times. If a table is experiencing an abnormal delay, a manager usually visits the kitchen to check on the status of their food, then communicates the estimated time of arrival to the server. But even when the server has no idea how much longer the wait will be, they may offer empty promises anyway, simply to defuse the situation.

WAITER SAYS: "Can I bring you anything else?"

TRANSLATION: It's time for you to ask for the check. We need your table back.

Restaurants never like asking guests to leave when they're "camping"—an industry term for lingering long after the meal has ended—but it can be problematic when a table that loiters causes other guests to wait. So once desserts have been cleared and coffees have been consumed, the staff may start sending subtle signals that it's time to go. There are rare occasions, if a table of campers doesn't get the hint, when managers will politely ask them to leave or offer to relocate them to the bar. Most of the time, though, if everyone is finished, the server will offer "Anything else?" as a gentle prompt to encourage the table to ask for the check. If the table declines the offer, it is acceptable for the server to discreetly deliver the bill. A mindful diner will pay promptly. If you've finished your meal and prefer to stay at the table for another round of after-dinner drinks, always ask your server if the table is needed before you start ordering digestifs.

WAITER SAYS: "I'm sorry, I couldn't get an authorization on your credit card."

TRANSLATION: Your credit card was declined, but I'm trying not to embarrass you in front of your friends by making it seem like a processing issue.

Believe me, it's just as awkward for your server to return a declined credit card as it is for you to have your card rejected (unless they dislike you, in which case it can be joyful). We're in the hospitality business, so we try to break the news to you gently by playing it off as a fluke occurrence, even though we have suspicions that you probably maxed out the card. If this happens, politely apologize and offer an alternative form of payment without making a big to-do about how the bank probably placed a hold on your card because you've been traveling a lot overseas lately. Nobody cares about your excuses. Hopefully, after your replacement card is approved, you'll overcompensate by leaving a huge tip to make sure there is no confusion about the state of your financial health.

THE TAKEAWAY

Waiters don't always say what they mean because honesty can be problematic in restaurant settings. With experience, guests can learn to read between the lines to better decipher the hidden message behind what servers are saying. Even something as simple as the waiter dropping a clue about the flavor profile of a particular dish might spare you from having to send it back. Training your ear to detect the nuances of waiter-speak will help you get the most out of your service experiences.

CHAPTER SEVEN

Why Restaurants Say No

When you say "yes" to others, make sure
you're not saying "no" to yourself.

—PAULO COELHO

When I worked at a rustic Italian trattoria in the early aughts, guests would regularly ask for a Caprese salad—sliced tomatoes with fresh mozzarella cheese and basil—even though most of the time we didn't offer a Caprese salad on the menu. "How can you call yourself an Italian restaurant when you don't serve Caprese salad?" guests would ask incredulously. The truth was that the restaurant *did* serve a Caprese salad—a very delicious one in fact—but the dish was only offered as a special during peak tomato season in late summer, when vibrant, colorful heirloom varieties could be consistently sourced from local farms. In the dead of winter, when only hothouse or imported tomatoes were available, the chefs were unwilling to offer an inferior version of the dish. I'd gently explain this to guests and recommend other seasonal alternatives. But many people simply could not accept the fact that the chef of an Italian restaurant wasn't willing to just "whip up" a Caprese using whatever tomatoes were available.

Of course, the chefs could have *easily* prepared a mediocre Caprese for any guests who wanted one, but doing so would've compromised their values. This scenario illustrates how a guest's needs can often be at odds with the restaurant's standards. Customers often don't know what's best for them, or they think they know better than the people running the establishment how it should operate. When restaurants enforce rules, they typically do so to maintain operational order. Allowing guests to dictate the rules invites chaos, and chaos often results in poor execution.

Unfortunately, when a restaurant denies a special request, even when its intentions are pure, it can be construed as inhospitable. Dogmatic service culture in the United States—such as Danny Meyer's enlightened hospitality—has reinforced the notion that restaurants should go to extraordinary lengths to satisfy their guests. Of course, all restaurateurs should strive to put their guests' needs first, but accommodating special requests can often create undesirable operational challenges.

Puritanical views toward hospitality like Meyer's may be admirable, but in the real world, adhering to the dogma often compounds the power imbalances that already exist between servers and guests. Try to imagine being in a relationship in which one person believes their needs should always come first. If that side always expects preferential treatment, the relationship is doomed to fail. Of course, a restaurant relationship is more transactional than a personal one; guests are paying hard-earned money in exchange for attentive service, but that doesn't change the fact that these relationships can collapse if they fall out of balance.

Too many guests get caught up in questions of right or wrong when they dine out. But the restaurant often views the same questions as a matter of what is fair or unfair. It helps when guests can accept that saying no is almost always the result of a restaurant's carefully thought-out decision about what works best for its business. The restaurant's goal is always to make customers happy, which often necessitates accommodating special requests, even when doing so causes unwanted disruptions in the flow of service. But every restaurant must know its own limits—the point at which being too accommodating can become problematic.

I've seen many situations when one table's needs usurp attention from other guests in the dining room while unnecessarily putting the staff under duress. When a table has a million special requests that require the server to go back and forth to the kitchen to specify how much salt to put on everyone's food or to find out which dishes are made with seed oils, it compromises the server's attentiveness to other guests.

Restaurants are like freight trains—you can't slow them down once they've started moving. If someone in the dining room pulls the emergency break, it's going to affect every other diner's experience. Creating a reasonable set of rules for guests to follow limits any unexpected variables that might cause the train to derail. As much as restaurants love saying yes to make guests happy, sometimes saying no is necessary to keep the trains running smoothly and on time.

As guests, we can help restaurants deliver better service to everyone by accepting our collective role in not only our table's successful dining experience but also the successful experiences of others. This often necessitates a willingness to accept that we might not always get our way. Ultimately, properly enjoying a restaurant requires trust and a belief that the people who created the restaurant always have your best interests in mind. That means accepting that even when they say no, they mean yes.

TRUST RESTAURANTS TO DO
THINGS THEIR WAY

The owner of a bar in Philadelphia that prides itself on sustainability told me recently that he doesn't offer dirty martinis with olives in his bar because olives can't be sourced locally. To serve olives, he would have to import them from thousands of miles away, which would violate the bar's commitment to only serving products—including its entire selection of craft spirits, beers, and wines—from east of the Mississippi River. Instead, the cocktail menu features a house version of a dirty martini served with seasonal pickles (such as one he makes with cherry tomatoes in summer). In lieu of the requisite olive juice, he adds a splash of the zesty pickle brine to make the cocktail dirty.

"Doesn't that upset a lot of your guests?" I asked him, referring to the absence of martini olives. "Of course it does," he told me. "But we hope that they'll trust us to serve them something that will make them happy." He insisted that most people who order the house dirty martini love it, but it isn't always easy to convince every guest to try something new. I'm guessing that many folks leave thinking that the bar's refusal to serve olives is self-righteous or that its unwillingness to make exceptions for olive lovers is inhospitable.

But I think there's a valuable lesson in all of this. As guests, we don't always get to shape every bar and restaurant into the image of what we want them to be. We should accept them for what they are. Furthermore, if we approach our restaurant experiences with an open mind, there's always a chance that we'll enjoy ourselves even more doing things their way than ours. As this bar owner understands, a dirty martini with a delicious house-made pickle can be much more exciting than having one with a sad, soggy olive that came from halfway around the world.

What's the Deal with Dress Codes?

There was a time when many upscale restaurants were "jackets required." These policies dictated that men and women would not be admitted without formalwear—suits or sports coats for men and dresses or skirts for women. Draconian measures like this are far less common today, but many restaurants still forbid guests from wearing shorts, ripped jeans, flip-flops, hats, athletic wear, or sneakers. *Business casual* or *cocktail attire* are terms commonly used to encourage formal dress without mandating it. Dress codes can be fraught, as recent controversies have shown how these policies tend to be discriminatory, often targeting people of color for their style choices. But in most cases, restaurants institute dress codes to curate a particular vibe. When an upscale restaurant goes to great lengths to create a luxurious atmosphere, it undermines that vision when people show up wearing baseball caps, tank tops, or yoga gear. These rules can be controversial, but they should be abided without protest. Think of it like being asked to remove your shoes when you enter a friend's home. It would be impolite to question why doing so is necessary or to refuse to remove them. You should approach restaurant visits with the same deference.

YOU CAN'T ALWAYS GET WHAT YOU WANT

When restaurants say no, it's often to protect guests from their own bad ideas. I can remember so many situations as a waiter where a guest would ask to remove a divisive ingredient from a dish—cilantro or anchovies, for example—then be dismayed when the dish comes out tasting bland or looking dull. It's probably not the greatest idea to ask if you can have a dish called "Lamb with Eggplant Three Ways" without eggplant. Unfortunately, many guests are certain they'll enjoy the dish anyway because they love lamb. I've seen countless people ignore the warnings and insist on making arbitrary changes to a dish, only to be utterly miserable with the results.

If guests aren't familiar with the menu, it's impossible for them to know which modifications will work and which won't. To some degree, the waiter's job is to protect guests from modifying dishes in ways that they know won't be successful. Requesting to swap a sauce from one dish for another or asking to remove dairy from a recipe to make it vegan may sound good in theory to someone who has never ordered these dishes before, but experienced waitstaff should know better whether such changes are feasible or not.

As annoying as it can be to hear chefs proselytize about how guests should enjoy their food, it's wrong-minded to think that restaurants should unconditionally accommodate every special request. Mindful guests should understand that chefs take enormous pride in their work and spend hours developing and perfecting recipes. It's disrespectful to all that effort when guests expect the chef to alter certain dishes from how they're intended to be served. *A restaurant chef is not a private chef.* If they refuse to accommodate a special request, there is usually a legitimate reason for why they won't do it. If so, then guests should respect the chef's decision without any blowback.

Many full-service restaurants have protocols around ordering that can seem austere but are often intended to manage the flow of orders into the kitchen. One common example is when guests are forbidden from ordering their appetizers separately from their entrées in traditional two-course fine dining restaurants. While some guests find these rules oppressive, the logic is quite simple. From the chef's perspective, it's impossible to serve every table in the dining room smoothly without a routine and predictable structure around how everyone orders their food. Certain main courses, like large steaks or double-cut chops, have lengthy cooking times. It's impractical for a table to wait until they've finished their Caesar salads to order a thirty-two-ounce porterhouse steak that takes forty-five minutes to cook. To arrive in a timely fashion, that steak should hit the grill immediately when the salads are ordered.

Ultimately, it's in a guest's best interest to place the whole order together. By soliciting complete orders, the chef is protecting diners from having to endure uncomfortable delays between courses. But more importantly, chefs do this to ensure their kitchens stay organized. As new orders come in, chefs must create a plan for their line cooks, without which the kitchen cannot stay organized and on task. If customers are allowed to order at their leisure, then it becomes impossible for a chef to design a cogent plan for preparing their food, resulting in more frequent mistakes and unnecessary delays in service.

Obstinate guests often push back when waiters solicit them for the complete order. "We don't want to be rushed," they proclaim, as though the server is trying to force them to order everything at once to speed up their meal. But even when the waiter assures them that they won't be rushed, it's still hard for some guests to understand why they can't order their food incrementally. The answer is simple: allowing every table to order piecemeal invites anarchy in the kitchen.

The same goes for seating incomplete parties. If someone has a reservation for four people but only three are present, most busy restaurants will refuse to seat the party until the fourth guest arrives, even if it means seating them past their reservation time. It's a nuisance for many people who don't like waiting at a noisy bar, but it's very logical from the maître d's perspective. If parties are seated incomplete, it can lead to unexpected delays in getting the table back for later reservations. In most cases, when the latecomers don't arrive until thirty or forty-five minutes after the original reservation time, the incomplete party will sit idly without ordering their food. If the table is rebooked, it likely won't be returned on time.

When restaurants insist on only seating complete parties, they do so because it's easier to predict how much time each party will occupy the table. The clock starts once everyone is seated. Every minute in a busy restaurant is precious, and having a table stuck in a holding pattern can result in their outlasting the expected turn time. That's why hosts and maître d's often give firm "out-by" times to incomplete parties who are seated late. If the restaurant is unable to get the table back in a timely manner, it will almost certainly result in difficulty seating later reservations punctually.

WITHOUT RULES, RESTAURANTS
DESCEND INTO CHAOS

Restaurants generally don't like making exceptions to rules because it sets a dangerous precedent. If the chef accommodates a special request on one visit—like removing mushrooms from a sauce because a guest doesn't like them—then that guest will expect the chef to prepare the same sauce without mushrooms on every subsequent visit. But there are times when the kitchen is too busy to customize everyone's sauces. If the chef refuses to repeat the favor, then the guest will invariably say: "They did it for me last time I was here! Why can't they do it for me again?" These guests are unlikely to accept that the changing circumstances affected the decision to accommodate the request one time but not the other. To avoid these complications, restaurants often set strict parameters about what requests can and can't be accommodated.

In a busy restaurant, being too accommodating can cause systems to malfunction. Restaurants often refuse to serve joiners, unannounced guests who want to join existing tables in progress, because doing so might disrupt the harmony of the physical space. Adding an extra chair for a joiner can clog traffic patterns in critical passageways, impeding the staff's ability to serve other tables as well as encroaching on the comfort of neighboring guests.

Hosts and maître d's also often refuse to accommodate joiners because seating them can cause delays in turning the table. The late-arriving guest may expect to order a full meal, which is a problem if the rest of the table is already on their desserts. Allowing the joiner to order additional food reduces the likelihood that the table will be returned at its expected time. That may not be a big issue toward the end of the night, at say 10:00 p.m., but if the joiner arrives during prime-time hours, seating them will make it harder to have their table ready for the next round of reservations.

Maintaining Order at the Pass

The nervous system of every restaurant kitchen is the long counter surface where every table's incoming order and outgoing food is organized and assembled, called "the pass." This is where every dish is given a final inspection before being shepherded into the dining room. Whenever a new table places its order, a printed ticket (what chefs often call a "dupe") comes up near the pass. An expediter, the individual who is tasked with orchestrating when food is fired, then promptly calls out the contents of each ticket to the line cooks. The boisterous call of a well-organized "expo" (short for *expediter*) bellowing out each new order has an almost musical cadence. They typically use shorthand abbreviations for menu items to keep the verbiage succinct. "Order in! One ork (orecchiette pasta), one black spag no heat (squid ink spaghetti, hold the Calabrian chiles), one strip bloody (New York strip steak, cooked rare), and one striper SOS (striped bass, sauce on the side)!" the expo shouts. As new orders roll in, they neatly arrange each new ticket on the pass to ensure an orderly firing process, being careful to hold back any tables that may be eating slowly. Without an experienced, detailed expediter, the pass can devolve into chaos, resulting in the kitchen sending out the wrong dishes, fire tickets with long delays, or improperly cooked food.

Ideally, a manager will offer to move the party to a larger, more comfortable table when a joiner arrives, but if one isn't available, pushing together random tables and cramming in extra chairs might overcrowd the space. I've seen many nightmare scenarios in which random people start showing up every half-hour wanting to join a table of friends, and every one of them expects to order more food on their own schedule. The minute you allow the first person to join, you're forced to keep allowing others who arrive later. It's a slippery slope, and being overly accommodating in these situations is a surefire way for staff to lose control of the dining room.

SUBSTITUTIONS ARE NOT
A ZERO-SUM GAME

You don't see as many restaurants printing NO SUBSTITUTIONS in big block letters on menus as often as they once did. But most restaurants, especially the fine dining ones, are still not very charitable about making them. On the surface, it seems inhospitable to deny guests what they want, but the truth is that allowing substitutions can be impractical in very tangible ways. The most obvious way relates to food costs. If a cheeseburger comes with French fries, the price of the dish on the menu accounts for French fries having a relatively low food cost. So, it doesn't make economic sense for a restaurant to allow everyone who doesn't like French fries to substitute truffle mashed potatoes or maple-glazed brussels sprouts for the same price when those items are more costly to make. Some restaurants may be willing to offer certain substitutions with a supplemental charge, but most guests will bristle at having to pay more.

There are often logistical reasons why chefs can't make substitutions. Most restaurant kitchens carefully par certain side items, garnishes, or sauces that are meant to accompany each dish. Ingredients need to be prepped in advance (brined, blanched, marinated, seasoned, and such), which can take hours in some cases. If the kitchen runs low on these items during service, they can't always be easily replenished. Allowing guests to order vegetables that are meant to accompany specific main courses as stand-alone side dishes, for example, might cause the kitchen to run out of these ingredients prematurely, meaning that parts of the menu will be "eighty-sixed," or "86'd" (industry parlance for sold out), depriving future guests of enjoying those items.

In these moments, it's important to remember that when you dine out in a restaurant, your decisions often have a direct impact on the other people dining around you. If a restaurant refuses to substitute the sweet corn polenta that comes with the braised beef short ribs as an alternative side dish for your roasted half-chicken, it's because they don't want to sell out of the polenta and risk disappointing someone else who orders the short ribs later. Never forget that it could be you on the losing end of this proposition, so try to show grace when substitutions aren't allowed. If every diner is mindful of this shared responsibility, then no one should ever leave disappointed.

THE TAKEAWAY

All restaurants have rules for a reason. When restaurants say no, there is almost always a carefully considered thought process behind the decision. Instead of challenging the staff's authority when you get a negative response, accept that these decisions are made with your best interests in mind. Respecting the rules will earn you respect in return, and your willingness to be a team player should result in servers reciprocating your generosity throughout the rest of your meal.

CHAPTER EIGHT

Managing Disappointing Experiences

If I'm brought the wrong order at a restaurant,
I don't send it back, because I don't want
the waiter to get mad at me.

—BETTY GILPIN

We've all been there before. Your main courses arrive, and everyone is about to dig in, but Grandma Rose's well-done grilled salmon with steamed vegetables is inexplicably missing. The table switches into panic mode, frantically searching for answers. Uncle Raymond flails his arms around like an inflatable tube man flopping in the wind outside a car dealership. Moments later, the server resurfaces, red-faced and clammy. He expresses remorse about the situation, mumbling inaudibly about how the kitchen is very busy and might've lost the salmon ticket. Either way, refiring a new dish will take at least ten minutes, and by the time it finally arrives, the experience is already ruined.

As a server, I've been on the receiving end of some epic tirades by irate customers. I've witnessed large parties leave in the middle of their appetizer course because a manager refused to lower the volume of the music. I've seen grown adults turn into cranky infants because they were charged for a dish they didn't like, even though they left nothing on the plate but crumbs. Regardless of the merits of their grievances, the outrage rarely fits the crimes. Aside from a negligent server whose ineptitude causes physical harm—like ignoring the severity of a food allergy and sending someone to the hospital—every mistake that happens in a restaurant is forgivable. No crisis should ever be beyond repair.

In my experience, when diners lose their cool, it's usually symptomatic of a deeper, more personal issue. I'm not a psychologist, but I see people carrying their emotional baggage into restaurants with them all the time. This is why servers abhor working on Hallmark holidays such as Valentine's Day, Mother's Day, and Father's Day. The pressure people feel to make these holidays extra special causes family drama to bubble over the surface in uncomfortable and ugly ways. In hospitality, carrying the burden for guests' emotional baggage is an everyday occurrence. Sometimes they've had a stressful day at work; maybe someone just lost their job or had a drag-out fight with a significant other or spouse. They might have a lack of chemistry with their tablemates, as for someone trapped in an argument with a drunk coworker or stuck on a miserable blind date.

There is a mindset within the industry (especially among those who adhere to the Danny Meyer school of hospitality) that restaurants should revel in these opportunities to "turn people around" with the power of great service. I have no doubt that engineering warm and fuzzy hospitality moments can be profound and meaningful, but perpetuating this kind of hospitality dogma often comes at a steep emotional and psychological cost for staff, who have to overcompensate for people's unhappiness. Servers are not mental health professionals, nor should they be expected to diagnose personal problems or administer therapy. Their job is to make people feel welcome and to provide friendly, efficient service. Too often, though, staff is expected to reverse the course of someone's terrible day and turn every frown upside down. But mindful guests are willing to share the burden when things go wrong and show grace to alleviate some of the pressure the staff feels to be perfect every time.

THE INEVITABILITY OF HUMAN ERROR

Mistakes happen in restaurants. Over my twenty-year career, I made hundreds, if not thousands, of them. Some are harmless and easily rectified, like forgetting to order a side dish or bringing the wrong garnish for a martini, and some have the capacity to totally obliterate someone's experience, like ordering grilled quail for a vegetarian. Once I ordered someone sixty oysters instead of six simply because I accidentally touched an extra key on the computer screen and didn't realize it. Needless to say, I was not in the chef's good graces that night. In another moment of haste, I misread my own handwriting and ordered someone the crabcakes instead of the snow crab legs. Even the most talented waiter will occasionally forget to put in a round of drinks or inadvertently order the wrong dish.

Every dining experience involves forfeiting some degree of control. When things go wrong, guests recognize how helpless they are. But dining successfully requires having a certain degree of faith that the staff always has your best interests in mind. As long as warm-blooded, sentient people operate restaurants and not AI-programmed robots, human error is unavoidable, even in three-star Michelin dining rooms. No matter how disciplined a staff is, there will always be occasional hiccups in service. It helps when the dining room is filled with patient and accommodating guests.

Aside from human error, most modern restaurants are also hardwired with glitchy technology that can malfunction at any given moment. Point-of-sale (POS) systems freeze in the middle of a busy night and need to be rebooted. Internet connections crash unexpectedly. When these things happen, it disrupts communication between the front and back of the house, making it more difficult to place new orders, fire food for tables when they're ready, and process credit card payments. The deadly combination of glitchy technology and human error can lead to some epic meltdowns.

There's a reason that waiting tables consistently appears at the top of every list of most stressful jobs. Restaurant visits are emotionally charged. The more money people spend, the higher the stakes are. Uplifting restaurant experiences etch themselves in our memories, but the memory of one negative experience often outlasts all the positive ones. You'll never forget the time a food runner dropped an entire tray of cream of asparagus soup into your lap or that arrogant French waiter in Provence, who condescended to everyone he identified as a tourist. Relationships are consummated or destroyed over restaurant meals. Business deals are won or lost. The human drama that plays out nightly inside the walls of a restaurant is a simmering cauldron of agony and ecstasy. The staff's job is to prevent the pot from spilling over.

By now, it should be clear what to expect when something goes wrong in a nice restaurant. A sharply dressed manager appears, profusely apologizing and offering restitution. But guests rarely give much thought to what they can do to help ameliorate an adverse situation. How someone responds to disappointment when they dine out can have a significant impact on whether an underwhelming restaurant experience can be resuscitated. If the staff is proactive about fixing a problem, then guests should be willing to move forward with the meal in a positive way without harboring resentment.

Mindful guests learn how to manage disappointment in nonadversarial ways. Anyone can be a great restaurant guest when the food is impeccable and service is flawless. But how you handle adversity in a restaurant is the true test of your dining literacy. Showing grace means that you acknowledge that restaurants are run on people power and that mistakes are unavoidable when there are fallible human beings cooking and serving your food.

RESTAURANTS AREN'T PERFECT— ENJOY THEIR IMPERFECTIONS

As a captain at one of the most popular steakhouses in New York City, I experienced what I consider to be one of the worst service disasters of my career. The restaurant was a destination for gargantuan trophy steaks, and we often featured limited quantities of high-end beef to tempt our corporate clientele dining on expense accounts. The astronomical prices boosted our check averages, but we mostly sold them for bragging rights, a constant competition among the staff for who could sell the most expensive cut.

One night, we were featuring various steaks from Snake River Farms in California. Snake River is renowned for its humanely raised cattle and limited organic production. We offered dry aged *côtes du boeuf* that evening—behemoth center-cut ribeye steaks meant to serve up to four people—starting at sixty ounces for five hundred dollars per steak. Around 8:00 p.m., I had a four-top of out-of-towners who clearly had no price constraints. "Is it worth it?" one of them asked. As I'd been trained, I brought over the steak board, a large marble tray covered with various hunks of crimson-red cow flesh artfully arranged with bouquets of fresh herbs and garlic bulbs, including the Snake River Farms ribeye I was recommending. It was like wheeling over a dessert cart for carnivores. The table didn't flinch when I quoted the price.

Thick steaks like this take forever to cook. It might be close to an hour from the time the table orders it for the finished steak to be delivered. The reason for the delay—as all professional cooks know—is because grilled meats need to rest. For the internal temperature to be more evenly distributed throughout the meat, steaks need to spend extended time resting off the grill. The larger the steaks are, the longer they need to be rested. If a steak is rushed, it will bleed when sliced and the meat won't be as tender. In this case, I warned the guests of the imminent delay at the outset and suggested a pasta middle course to bide the time.

About ten minutes after their pastas had been cleared, I heard a thunderous crash across the dining room. I looked over toward the kitchen, where a food runner was looking down at a collapsed tray on the floor in horror. Next to the pile of mashed potatoes splattered on the carpet and the proprietary steak sauce splashed all over the kitchen doors lay my table's precious five-hundred-dollar Snake River Farms ribeye. My pulse momentarily stopped. The dining room went silent.

Like paramedics, the staff immediately went into triage mode. My manager explained the situation to the guests, offering to refire another steak as soon as possible. Because it would take at least another forty-five minutes to cook, we offered to open another bottle of wine, the same two-hundred-dollar bottle they were enjoying, with our compliments. They took the news graciously and even expressed concern that the poor food runner who had dropped the tray might lose his job. In the end, they didn't power trip or demand more than we offered in damages. The second steak finally arrived, and they loved it, laughing about the absurdity of the whole situation.

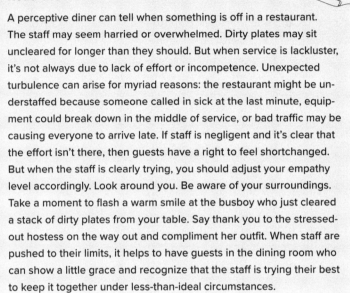

Read the Room

A perceptive diner can tell when something is off in a restaurant. The staff may seem harried or overwhelmed. Dirty plates may sit uncleared for longer than they should. But when service is lackluster, it's not always due to lack of effort or incompetence. Unexpected turbulence can arise for myriad reasons: the restaurant might be understaffed because someone called in sick at the last minute, equipment could break down in the middle of service, or bad traffic may be causing everyone to arrive late. If staff is negligent and it's clear that the effort isn't there, then guests have a right to feel shortchanged. But when the staff is clearly trying, you should adjust your empathy level accordingly. Look around you. Be aware of your surroundings. Take a moment to flash a warm smile at the busboy who just cleared a stack of dirty plates from your table. Say thank you to the stressed-out hostess on the way out and compliment her outfit. When staff are pushed to their limits, it helps to have guests in the dining room who can show a little grace and recognize that the staff is trying their best to keep it together under less-than-ideal circumstances.

CHAOS IS THE NATURAL STATE OF A RESTAURANT

With so many variables at play simultaneously—a dining room full of hungry people with high expectations, an overworked kitchen staff who were out partying the night before, menu changes that were rushed without sufficient time for fine-tuning—entropy is inevitable. Unfortunately, what makes restaurants so thrilling is also what makes them imperfect. Having to juggle so many unpredictable variables at once to mitigate the chaos makes restaurant work unnervingly stressful compared with most conventional jobs. Guests' behavior is the most unpredictable part, and something as simple as a table of guests taking a twenty-minute smoke break outside unannounced while their food is ready only amplifies the chaos.

Restaurant meals can't be perfect every time. Of course, restaurants should always go to great lengths to provide a seamless experience for their guests, but even the finest restaurants in the world have bad days. It's no different from every other industry, but for some reason, the tolerance for imperfection is much lower when it comes to dining out. If guests can learn to better manage their tolerance for these imperfections, they will boost their chances of leaving happy.

NOBODY WINS THE BLAME GAME

I can't tell you how many times as a waiter I served guests who insisted that they had ordered a dish one way when I was certain they had ordered it another. Unfortunately, there's no way to play back a recording of the conversation to reveal which party is responsible for the miscommunication. Servers are conditioned to accept blame, in part because arguing with paying customers is a losing proposition. Restaurant managers generally expect staff to be docile, to avoid offending guests, regardless of whose fault it is. Playing the blame game is certain to sour a guest's experience, so hospitality professionals are trained to take the high road.

Guests that receive the wrong food might say, "I'm pretty sure I ordered this with a baked potato, and they gave me French fries instead." While it may very well be the server's or chef's mistake, once the mistake is made, it doesn't really matter who's fault it is. When this happens, the most important thing is to communicate that you wanted a baked potato. You can convey this without the need to lay blame or disparage the staff. A better way to phrase it would be: "So sorry, I wanted this to come with a baked potato, but it came with French fries. Could you please have the kitchen fix it for me?"

It helps to approach every problem with the attitude that you share responsibility for what went wrong, even when you think it wasn't your fault. The truth is that guests don't always speak clearly about what they want, so occasionally vital information can be lost in translation. But regardless of who's right or wrong, it isn't productive to blame the server, especially when you can't always be sure that it's their fault.

DON'T SHOOT THE MESSENGER

When I waited tables, it was always frustrating when a popular menu item would sell out at the precise moment that one of my tables wanted to order it. All restaurants have limited inventory, so it's quite common to eighty-six popular menu items throughout the night. Whenever this happened, I'd express my sincerest apologies and offer alternatives, but no matter how remorseful I was, a small percentage of guests would be inconsolable. Some might even imply that I hadn't acted quickly enough to place the order on their behalf. "Are you sure there are no more left?" they'd ask incredulously. "How can it already be sold out at 9:00 p.m.?" I'd offer my sympathies again, but for whatever reason, some guests would still treat me like I was responsible.

When your food is taking too long—something that happens regularly in every restaurant—it's rarely the server's fault. The kitchen may be slammed with too many orders at once, or it might be understaffed because someone had a family emergency. It's possible that the server might have forgotten to fire your next course, but they aren't ever back in the kitchen cooking your food. Try not to be too hard on front-of-house staff when the pace of your meal is dragging. It's much more likely a kitchen issue and not their fault.

When guests lose control over their emotions, they can't engage in constructive dialogue about how to rectify the situation. Even though it's likely that the server is not solely to blame, angry guests tend to lash out at servers, assuming they were negligent. Becoming aggressive may yield results, in the form of comped items or extras from the kitchen, but it also reflects poorly on the guest and damages their relationship with the staff.

It's natural to feel upset when a restaurant experience disappoints, but the disappointment shouldn't obscure the fact that the staff is still trying hard to make you happy, even when things go wrong. The core of a server's job is to be a guardian for your table. When mistakes happen, most servers take it personally and will do whatever they can to make it right. Attacking them or becoming aggressive undermines those efforts.

WELL-DONE BUT JUICY

I remember once being on the receiving end of a breathless tirade by a French guest who was irate that his well-done filet mignon was too dry. Filet mignon is a lean cut of beef, so chefs rarely cook it to more than medium. After a few bites, the Frenchman called me over to the table, pointed to the charred lump of meat, and pressed down on it to demonstrate the lack of meat juices emanating from inside. I didn't say a word.

He began to lecture me on the temperature scale that French people use to measure the level of doneness in meat. In France, he explained, there are four basic ways to order steak. *Bleu* means very rare, quickly seared on both sides. *Saignant*, literally meaning "bloody," is a bit more cooked than *bleu* but still quite rare. *À point* implies "perfectly cooked" (closest to the American ideal of medium rare), and *bien cuit* signifies well-done. The lifeless steak in front of him was not *bien cuit*, the Frenchman explained, looking back at me as though I was supposed to thank him for his impromptu TED talk on how to properly cook steak.

"Do you want to taste it?" he said, with a belligerent lilt. "Maybe then you will believe me?" He broke one of my cardinal rules: *never offer a server your half-eaten leftovers*. That will not help the server believe you. "Ask the chef if he thinks this is a proper well-done filet mignon!" he insisted. I swiftly removed the plate, apologized that the steak was not to his liking, and offered to bring him something else. But he was adamant that the chef should prepare him another steak to a proper well-done— by his standards, of course. I could already picture the chef having a nuclear meltdown the moment I entered the kitchen with this man's untouched steak in my hands. "Table 14 wants another filet. *Well-done but juicy*, chef," I'd say with a wry smile, moments before being thrown out of the kitchen.

I've had countless guests complain when their steaks were served too rare, but this was the first time that I'd ever had someone say that a well-done steak was *too well-done.* The wiring inside my waiter's brain was short-circuiting. I carried the dish back to the kitchen, bracing for the chef's wrath. You could almost hear his blood pressure rising as he stared blankly at the desiccated beef on the plate. "What does he want?" the chef asked, sounding exasperated. "I won't cook another filet mignon well-done for this guy." So, I returned to the table and politely conveyed to the Frenchman that the chef would be happy to refire his steak. I chose to omit the part about how I asked the chef to cook the second steak medium-well instead.

The whole ordeal reminded me how often in hospitality we're expected to show deference to people who are misinformed or, like Monsieur Bien Cuit, hold beliefs about cooking that clash with the restaurant's way of doing things. Servers have the unenviable job of acting as arbitrators in these situations. Most guests don't appreciate how lucky they are to have servers acting as proxies for their needs in the kitchen, shielding them from the fury of a prideful chef. Ultimately, the need to have a reliable buffer between hungry guests and angry chefs may prevent automated technology from ever totally usurping human servers in restaurants. Chefs will always need someone to yell at.

SENDING FOOD BACK THE RIGHT WAY

Years ago, I worked at a fine dining restaurant in Midtown Manhattan that was a destination for high-powered executives and financiers to consummate multimillion-dollar deals over obscenely expensive Cobb salads. During the Mad Men era of the 1950s, the iconic space was once a dramatic backdrop for three-martini lunches and steamy office affairs. Corporate types behave much more conservatively today, but the dining room is still regularly filled with billionaire CEOs, real estate moguls, and venture capitalists who thrive on fraternizing in a palatial setting over thirty-five-dollar burgers and iced teas, where they can semi-privately talk shop.

When I worked there, we had one lunch regular who dined in the restaurant daily, arriving like clockwork at 11:45 a.m. and ordering a vodka martini on the rocks with extra ice on the side. The staff shuddered the moment he paced through the entrance with his signature scowl. No matter what, we knew that there was at least an 80 percent chance that he would send most, if not all, of his food back. He typically ordered a burger with a level of specificity about how he liked it cooked that strayed from the standard temperature scale. When he inevitably complained about his meal, he'd add a slanderous remark about the people responsible for cooking it. "Don't those people learn how to cook a hamburger in culinary school?" he'd say with a grunt. "Or I guess these people didn't go to culinary school."

It was clear to the staff, after having to care for this miserable man day in and day out, that he was psychologically damaged. He seemed to revel in belittling people, something that might have been an effective tactic in business but likely wreaked havoc in his personal life. Had he approached his food complaints more constructively and with a modicum of respect, the staff would have showed more grace to him in return. But most days, we reciprocated his lack of regard, delivering the bare minimum level of service, which was what he deserved. Not only was he someone who had little respect for restaurant workers, but he was also a terrible tipper.

There are many unfounded urban myths about chefs retaliating against people who send their food back by returning it tainted. To some degree, a culture of fear still exists about giving chefs negative feedback that prompts some people to add the disclaimer "I don't want to upset the chef" whenever they have an issue with their food. The truth is, most chefs I've worked with—including those with acute anger management issues—simply want guests to be happy. Restaurant kitchens are too busy for chefs to be vindictive all the time, and it makes their lives much easier when customers enjoy their meal.

When you do have a problem with your food, the most important thing is to keep the conversation focused on the specifics of what's wrong. If the dish you ordered is too salty for your taste, summon the waiter, convey that you think the dish is over-seasoned, and politely ask for a replacement. At this point, there is no need for any additional editorial remarks. As I pointed out earlier, assigning blame is also unnecessary; instead, treat your server respectfully, and be clear about how they can fix the problem.

Well-trained servers should offer guidance when you send back your food, to help minimize the disruption in your meal. Overcooked steaks and chops are difficult to refire quickly. In this case, the server might suggest ordering something else like grilled fish or a pasta that has a shorter cooking time. Ideally, accept one of the suggested alternatives, but if you prefer to have your dish remade, then it's incumbent upon you to accept that it can't be rushed. If you're bothered by the wait, ask the server if they can send you something to snack on like more bread or a dish of olives, so you don't feel awkward sitting with no food on the table while your tablemates are enjoying their meal.

You should never feel bad about sending food back in a restaurant, provided you have a legitimate grievance. In my opinion, it's always worse to say nothing because then you haven't given the restaurant the opportunity to remedy the situation. Chefs may not always agree with your complaints about the food, but you still have the right to make them without fear of retribution. As long as you present your complaints concisely without any animosity, then the staff should be happy to take whatever steps necessary to rectify the situation.

KEEP CALM AND CARRY ON

When bad restaurant experiences turn ugly, it's usually because the aggrieved party lets their grievances fester, until the pressure builds up to a nuclear explosion. Instead of inquiring about their missing food after twenty minutes, some guests wait for a half-hour or more before going postal. Ultimately, it's your responsibility to control your emotions as a guest, which also means that you might have to accept a resolution that isn't ideal.

Servers appreciate when guests remain calm during bouts of turbulence. Whenever the staff is visibly overwhelmed, you should try to downshift your expectations and raise your patience threshold. Making a fuss about your food taking too long when *everybody's* food is taking too long is pointless, like honking your horn incessantly when you're stuck in bumper-to-bumper traffic. Becoming aggressive with restaurant staff is belittling, even when you have a right to be mad. It implies that you think the staff is incompetent or that servers aren't committed to doing their jobs well, neither of which is likely true.

THE TAKEAWAY

We all wish that every restaurant experience could be perfect every time, but the reality is they aren't. Disappointment is unavoidable. Mindful guests show grace in the face of adversity. At the end of the day, you're just having dinner. No matter how high your expectations are going in, dining out in a restaurant isn't a matter of life or death. Restaurant experiences are supposed to be fun, and you can still find ways to enjoy yourself even when the food or service doesn't live up to your standards.

CHAPTER NINE

Troubleshooting and Triage

Don't dwell on what went wrong.
Instead focus on what to do next. Spend your energies
on moving forward toward finding the answer.

—DENIS WAITLEY

I must confess, I do not always live up to my own lofty standards as a restaurant guest. Sadly, I'm susceptible to the same destructive impulses as everyone else. So, when restaurant service is lackluster, sometimes I lose my cool too. My father had a short temper and could be abusive toward servers when he felt food or service hadn't lived up to his expectations. Witnessing his caustic behavior toward waitstaff and having been on the receiving end of countless tirades from irate guests myself as a server imbues me with deep empathy for service professionals. But I am not perfect.

Years ago, while dining with a former girlfriend and her family, I was unnecessarily rude to the staff, an experience that I still reflect upon with deep regret over ten years later. It was my job to pick the restaurant, and I'd invested a lot of time and energy into finding the right place. We were in Hawaii, so naturally it needed to be a restaurant that specialized in seafood. Even though I wasn't paying for dinner, I felt pressure for everything to go smoothly. I desperately wanted to impress her parents by choosing a restaurant they would love, and I indirectly transferred that pressure to the restaurant and its staff.

Along with individual appetizers, we ordered a dozen oysters for the table to share that were missing when our first course arrived. The staff was very busy, so we couldn't convey to our server right away that the oysters had been forgotten. By the time we'd finished our appetizers, we finally flagged down the server to alert her to our missing oysters. She apologized and promised to rush them to the table. I'd hoped that she would ask the chef to hold the fire on our main courses to allow us time to enjoy the oysters, but our entrées arrived before the oysters did. I could feel my skin getting hot. My girlfriend loved oysters, and she was really excited about ordering them. No one wants to eat ice-cold, refreshing oysters alongside piping hot main courses.

A few bites into our mains, a food runner approached us with the oysters and attempted to put them down in the middle of the table. Incensed that they had taken so long, I curtly instructed the food runner to take them away. My girlfriend pleaded with me to calm down, and I could see her parents shifting around in their seats, looking uncomfortable with how I'd handled the situation. Moments later, the server returned with the same tray of oysters, as though we'd mistakenly returned them. I objected again. "We really don't want to eat cold oysters with hot main courses!" I said sternly. "Would *you*?" As a waiter, I always hated it when guests asked rude, rhetorical questions like this. It's so condescending. I was behaving exactly like the guests I routinely condemned, only able to focus on my grievances and not on making the best out of a frustrating situation. Feeling annoyed and defeated, the server slumped back into the kitchen, undoubtedly to incur the wrath of the chef.

While it's true that the restaurant had screwed everything up with the timing of our oysters, I was the one who ended up looking more foolish in the end. There are any number of reasons why the mistake could've been made, but in the moment, I could only focus on how humiliated I felt because I had picked a restaurant that couldn't serve a simple tray of oysters at the right time. This kind of mistake probably happens to one out of every one hundred tables, but my lingering anxiety about the situation bubbled over to the point where I lost my cool and became nasty with the staff. I was worried about impressing my girlfriend's parents, but I ended up handling the situation in such a way that it reflected more poorly on me than it did the restaurant. If I could go back in time, I certainly would've handled the situation more empathetically and made a better effort to keep my emotions in check.

No one enjoys the feeling of having a special evening in a restaurant compromised by mistakes with food or service. It's easy to get upset when things go wrong, especially when expectations run high. But mindful guests can assist with rescue and recovery operations, simply by being more patient and empathetic. It's important to be able to step back when things get heated, take a deep breath, survey the situation, and figure out how you can make the most of it. There's an art to reclaiming negative restaurant experiences. Here I'll discuss some common scenarios that occur in restaurants and how to deal with them properly.

WHAT TO DO WHEN SOMETHING YOU ORDERED IS TAKING TOO LONG

I'll never forget how hard it was to work in restaurants in the aftermath of September 11, 2001. I'd recently started working as a waiter in a well-known Italian restaurant in downtown Manhattan when the towers fell. The restaurant closed on the day of the attack, like most places in the New York City area did on 9/11, but to the staff's surprise, it reopened the next day with limited hours. There were military blockades and security checkpoints that restricted access to the street where the restaurant was located. Rescue crews and first responders were working tirelessly around the clock to search for any signs of life. The indelible smell of molten steel and burning jet fuel, so familiar to people who lived through 9/11 in New York City, still permeated the air.

As much as I vividly recall the horrors of living in the city during such a tumultuous time, I also remember a lot about how customers in the restaurant behaved in the ensuing days. The majority of guests were gracious and truly appreciated the sacrifices that many of us had made to welcome them. But there were others who refused to adjust their attitude to meet the moment, entering with the same sense of entitlement they felt under normal circumstances. But obviously, these were not normal circumstances.

I remember one table, a couple who'd ordered a very rare bottle of Sassicaia, a Tuscan red wine, that cost around five hundred dollars. We weren't very busy, for obvious reasons, so staffing was very light. Normally, we had two sommeliers on the floor at any given time. But with a skeleton crew, there was only one sommelier that night, which made it hard for him to retrieve bottles from the cellar in a timely manner. After ten minutes had passed with no sign of the table's wine, the gentleman who ordered it called me over to the table to complain.

"I'm so sorry for the delay," I said, as warmly as I could under the circumstances. "Your wine should be arriving any moment, sir." After another five minutes passed with no sign of their bottle, the couple was looking around in a panic. By then, their first course had already arrived, and the man summoned me over to the table with a raised hand like he was hailing a taxi. "Is there a reason why we don't have our wine yet?" he asked, taking a more aggressive tone. "I'm happy to switch to something by the glass if you don't want me to spend so much money." As he became increasingly upset, other guests in the vicinity looked on in disbelief. The staff was incredulous. With the wreckage of the World Trade Center buildings still smoldering a few miles away, none of us could understand how this man believed that waiting fifteen minutes for a bottle of wine was proper cause for becoming belligerent with the staff.

Under normal circumstances, his behavior might be justified. But restaurant guests should be sensitive to what's happening around them and adjust their attitude to suit the situation. In this case, the man who ordered the wine was insensitive to the context—that it was virtually impossible to run a restaurant normally under such tragic circumstances—and certainly could have been more compassionate about the delay in his wine service.

But this gentleman's conduct illustrates how some guests are not able to see outside themselves and their own needs. Whenever you dine out, you should always be prepared for the possibility that service can be slow or that a restaurant will be busier than it can handle. Most great restaurants find a way to rise to the occasion, but if they're unable to, for whatever reason, mindful guests should be able to adjust their expectations accordingly.

There are always preemptive measures guests can take to help mitigate avoidable hiccups. If you have a time constraint, for example, always make note of it on your reservation and alert the server the moment you sit down. If you aren't pressed for time but you're noticing that your food is delayed, flag down the server the moment the delay becomes palpable. Letting your impatience fester often leads to more explosive outbursts if the delays persist. You should never wait more than twenty minutes in between courses. If you hit the twenty-minute mark after your appetizers have been cleared and there's still no sign of your entrées, politely summon the server to ask if they can check on your food. It helps to frame these concerns with conciliatory phrases like "we know you're super busy" or "we're not in a hurry or anything." If you reach the thirty-minute mark and your food still hasn't arrived, then asking to speak with the manager is justified.

HOW TO HANDLE RUDE OR
NEGLIGENT SERVICE

I recently dined with a friend at the crowded bar of a trendy Middle Eastern restaurant in Brooklyn. From the moment we sat down, my dining companion and I could tell that our bartender was having an off night. If you've worked in restaurants, it's easy to recognize when a server or bartender is in bad spirits because you've fought through similar feelings during service many times yourself. No matter how much you expect staff to always be on their A game, they're only human and have good days and bad days like everyone else. Servers can administer great service in a terrible mood or terrible service in a great mood, but not every server will be able to put on a happy face for every customer every night. How people behave in these situations as guests and the sensitivity they show to the staff's disposition can either exacerbate the problem or help to ameliorate it.

That night, the bartender ignored us for at least five minutes from the time we took our seats. I could feel my dining companion growing restless, but I assured her that flagging him down to order drinks was a bad idea. It was worth being patient for a few extra minutes, I told her, to allow him to greet us on his own terms. "I think we'd like to try some of your featured cocktails," I said, when he finally came over to greet us, "but we could use your help making our choices." I purposely avoided using the word *order* while discussing our drinks, which can sound pushy or aggressive when staff are feeling sensitive. Rather than saying you'd like to order drinks, it's better to say you'd like to "try" something or to express that you need help deciding. This makes the dialogue between you feel more collaborative.

In my experience, it helps to make your server feel needed in these instances when you sense that they're disengaged or irritated. I threw out a few softball questions about the cocktail list to demonstrate that I valued his input and expertise. Even though I had my eye on a different drink, I went along with his recommendation for a refreshing cocktail made with a special kind of Persian mint I'd never heard of before. He appreciated that I followed his advice, and I thoroughly enjoyed his recommendation.

After chatting with the bartender more as our meal progressed, we learned that moments before we arrived, another bar guest had acted disrespectfully toward one of his coworkers. The altercation left the staff feeling flustered. In the moment, the bartender wasn't able to focus his attention on the new guests at the bar because he was still so shaken by what had transpired. Once he explained the circumstances to us, his earlier standoffishness made sense. After we showed empathy for what had happened and built up a rapport together, his attitude changed dramatically. Had we been pushy about our needs initially, we might not have been able to have the breakthrough we did.

Not every situation with a rude server or bartender can be salvaged by solidarity. There are times when asking to speak to the manager to discuss unfriendly or negligent service is warranted. But this should always be a last resort. If you decide to lodge a formal complaint to management in the moment, you should ask the host or the maître d' who seated you, or someone other than the "problem" server, to send the manager to the table.

When complaints like this occur, the manager will usually assign a new server to your table, hoping that you'll get along better. The truth is: sometimes the chemistry between certain servers and guests simply doesn't click. When you dine out, you don't get to choose your server, and your server doesn't get to choose you. But there's really no reason to suffer through it if it isn't a good match. Even the most attentive servers who regularly receive positive feedback will occasionally have a table that finds them unhelpful or rude.

Keeping the mindset that it's a chemistry issue and not incompetence is important. Have you ever gone to a hair salon when your normal stylist isn't available? You could get the same quality haircut from someone else, but the experience doesn't feel the same. Or sometimes you see a different stylist, and you find that you like them even more. Not every waiter has the right personality for every table. As a server, I would occasionally ask my managers to remove me from a table when I sensed chemistry issues. My managers usually preferred I soldier through it, but in most cases, having a fresh face serve the table alleviated the tension and ended up enhancing the guests' experience.

WHAT TO DO WHEN YOU HAVE
A WOBBLY TABLE

Sitting down to a rickety table can be unnerving. Whatever you do, try to resist the urge to repair the issue yourself. There's no need to Mac-Gyver the table base with sugar packets, scrunched-up cocktail napkins, or matchbooks. It's always more prudent to ask a staff member to fix the table for you. Wobbly tables are often caused by warped flooring. If that's the case, the staff often knows how to reposition the table to fix the problem. Many restaurant tables are fitted with adjustable feet that screw into the bottom of the legs, which can be raised and lowered to make minor adjustments on the fly. For temporary fixes, many restaurants also carry "wobble wedges," small plastic shims that can be easily inserted under the table to help stabilize it with minimal intrusion.

HOW TO COMMUNICATE THAT
YOU DON'T WANT TO BE RUSHED

Within the constraints of running a profitable business, great restaurants should do everything they can to allocate as much time as possible for each table to enjoy a leisurely meal. Unfortunately, the customer and the restaurant are not always aligned about what constitutes an appropriate amount of time to occupy the table.

If the circumstances warrant communicating to the staff that you'd like to slow down the pace of your meal—if you and your dining companions haven't seen each other in a long time, for example—there are ways of doing it tactfully. The biggest mistake that guests make, which drives servers crazy, is declaring, "We don't want to be rushed!" the moment they sit down. This approach positions the guest in an adversarial role, which can make it harder to build solidarity with the staff throughout their meal.

A better approach would be to wait until you've placed the food order to discuss the pacing of your meal with your server. Ideally, give a little time to allow your relationship with the server to develop before you start making demands about slowing things down. This also ensures that your request is fresh in the server's mind when they send your order to the kitchen. To alert the chef, the waiter will often attach a note to the top of your order ticket that says, "Go slow" or "Wait for fire" or something else that calls attention to the fact that your table does not want to be rushed. In busy restaurants, servers are typically under enormous pressure to turn tables. Making demands that suggest that you feel entitled to occupy the table as long as you want can ruffle a server's feathers unnecessarily.

You should never expect to have complete control over the pacing of your meal. At the end of the day, you need to have faith that the restaurant will do its best to give you ample time to enjoy the experience. But kitchen systems are extremely regimented, and holding orders in the kitchen for too many tables at once can cause tickets to pile up. Chefs often need to fire food on a brisk schedule to make room for all the new orders that are constantly pouring into the kitchen. A restaurant kitchen simply can't function properly if it allows every table to dictate the pace of their meal.

If it still feels like your food is coming out too quickly after you've requested to slow down, it might help to speak with the manager about it in a nonconfrontational way. In most cases, the manager has more clout in the kitchen than servers do when it comes to convincing the chef to give your table a little extra time in between courses.

HOW TO PROPERLY SEND BACK
A BOTTLE OF WINE

When a server or sommelier opens the bottle of wine you ordered and pours you a taste, it isn't meant as a way for you to evaluate whether you like it or not. The tasting ritual is designed to give the person who ordered it an opportunity to identify any flaws, such as the wine being "corked" (a taint caused by mold spores in the cork that can impart an off-putting, wet newspaper–like smell to the wine) or "cooked" (a condition that typically results from poor storage in which a wine loses its freshness). When you approve the wine, it *should* mean that you think the bottle is sound, not necessarily that you think it's good.

If you do find a flaw with the wine, alert a member of the staff as quickly as possible. Once you've communicated your issue, the staff will usually examine the bottle to verify your concerns. Most restaurants will replace the bottle without protest, even if they don't agree with your assessment. When a bottle is very expensive, however, the cost of replacing it may be prohibitive. Rather than risk having another bottle rejected, the staff may try to guide you into choosing a different wine. If you encounter any resistance about replacing an expensive bottle, be as flexible as you can about accepting suggested alternatives.

If the wine is sound but you aren't enjoying it, there are healthy ways of communicating your displeasure to the staff that will make them more willing to open something else for you. If you selected the bottle and you don't like it, you should never assume that a restaurant will automatically replace it. Even though most wine is heavily marked up, the wholesale cost is still very high, so restaurants can't afford to keep opening random bottles until guests find one they like. Having said that, it's also not in a restaurant's best interest to have guests drinking wine they aren't enjoying.

If the server or sommelier recommended a bottle that you aren't crazy about, it's more acceptable to send the wine back. If you do, it helps to be contrite and acknowledge that you shared in the decision to open the bottle they suggested. A productive way to approach it would be to call the person who recommended the wine over to the table and say: "I'm so sorry, but this wine isn't really what we were expecting. Would it be possible for us to choose something else?"

Anytime you send wine back, start by expressing what you didn't like about the wine, in as clear terms as possible. Be specific and try to focus on your expectations and not about the quality of the wine itself. Sommeliers invest a lot of time and effort in their wine programs, and it can be insulting when guests criticize the quality of the wines on the list. It's much more effective to use language like "I was really hoping for something more full-bodied and earthy, but I find this wine a little too fruit forward for my taste" rather than "We don't really love this bottle—the finish is pretty flat."

HOW TO HANDLE FINDING A
HAIR IN YOUR FOOD

Nothing can destroy an enjoyable dining experience faster than someone finding a hair in their food. But until hairless robots assume the cooking duties in every restaurant kitchen, there will always be a possibility that an errant eye lash or a strand of someone's locks could end up in your chopped salad. Most health departments mandate that cooks wear head coverings to minimize the risk of contamination, but even when kitchen staff is fastidious about keeping their heads covered, stray hairs may still randomly find their way onto guests' finished plates.

It can be very startling when you find hair in your food, but try to stay calm. Most of the time, it's a matter of bad luck rather than bad hygiene. It can be hard to focus on solutions when you feel grossed out, but the situation cannot be remedied unless you keep your cool. The server should immediately remove the plate and offer their sincere apologies. In most cases, they will ask you if you would like the kitchen to remake the dish or if you would like to order something else. If you've lost your appetite, feel free to say so. Obviously, the dish in question should always be removed from the bill, no questions asked. In most cases, management will also send extra desserts or other complimentary items to make it up to the guest.

WHAT TO DO IF THERE'S
A VERMIN SIGHTING

Years ago, I was working in a restaurant that underwent a massive renovation to build a state-of-the-art wine cellar. The building was over a hundred years old, and when construction began, the excavation process disturbed the rodent population on the entire block. For almost a year before the cellar was completed, the restaurant struggled with vermin infestations. Some of the rats in the basement could have easily been mistaken for raccoons. No amount of exterminator visits could keep the issue in check. Meanwhile, the kitchen was immaculate, but the physical structure surrounding it was not.

Some of the cleanest restaurants I've worked in have had cockroach problems, and some of the dirtiest ones didn't. But regardless, any time you see a cockroach scurry across the dining room floor, it's natural, as a restaurant guest, to assume that the establishment has a cleanliness issue. But evidence of vermin doesn't necessarily mean a restaurant is dirty. In fact, these issues are often caused by what's going on in the area around the restaurant more than by what's going on inside the restaurant itself.

If your table has a vermin sighting, report it to the staff immediately. If you've lost your appetite and don't wish to continue your meal, ask to speak to the manager and calmly express your desire to leave. In many cases, management will comp the full check, but you should always be prepared to pay for any items that you consumed before the incident. If you leave feeling that management didn't properly compensate you, save your grievances for the following day. A strongly worded email expressing that you're dissatisfied with the resolution or a phone call the next morning is much more effective than arguing about it at the table in a highly emotional state. It's also much easier for management to give full attention to your grievances without the distraction of a dining room filled with other guests.

Even though the sight of mice or bugs in a restaurant can be disturbing, some species are worse than others. Fruit fly infestations, for example, are preventable and can be a sign of standing water left in sink areas or perishable items like cocktail garnishes left uncovered behind the bar. On the other hand, "nature bugs" like beetles or ladybugs may come from floral arrangements or decorative plants in the dining room and shouldn't provoke the same level of outrage.

HOW TO DEAL WITH TABLEMATES
MISTREATING STAFF

It can be very uncomfortable to dine with someone who doesn't treat the waitstaff respectfully. It may be a rude family member who always misbehaves in a restaurant, a work colleague you just met at a business dinner, or a blind date gone bad. In business settings in which groups have established hierarchies, workplace politics can make it difficult to speak out about an abusive colleague. Not everyone is willing to risk their job by telling their new boss that they're acting inappropriately. But even when the interpersonal dynamics at the table are complicated, mindful guests should be willing to acknowledge the problem with the server on the receiving end of the bad behavior.

If a tablemate is behaving irreverently, there are discreet ways to handle the situation that needn't be confrontational. If you can't address the issue directly with the offender, the best thing to do would be to approach your server away from the table, preferably out of view of your tablemates, to apologize on their behalf. Servers are usually too busy for a long-drawn-out emotional conversation, so keep the remarks as brief as possible. Say something like: "I just wanted to apologize for the way my coworker has been treating you tonight. His behavior does not speak for the rest of us, who really appreciate your service." Acknowledging that the rest of your party is cognizant of your tablemate's poor behavior and taking ownership of it can go a long way toward defusing the situation.

IS IT ACCEPTABLE TO LEAVE EARLY IF A DINING EXPERIENCE IS TERRIBLE?

Occasionally, a bad restaurant experience can get so bad that it's beyond reclamation. If you reach that threshold, there's really no reason to prolong the agony. That said, aborting a restaurant experience midway through your meal should always be a last resort. But if you sense irreconcilable differences—like staff members are consistently rude or the food is clearly not fresh—there are ways to tactfully extricate yourself from the situation.

If you do decide to pull the rip cord, always make sure a manager or maître d' supervises the unwinding process. No matter how aggrieved you feel, you should be willing to pay for everything that you've consumed up until that point. Under no circumstances should you ever leave without paying (unless management gives you permission). If the next course is on the way when you decide to leave, you should ask for the rest of the food to be wrapped to avoid it going to waste. Being disappointed with your experience does not justify wasting food or forcing the restaurant to eat the cost of your meal. Ultimately, it's always up to the management's discretion to decide whether or not to comp any portion of the bill or the entire check.

THE TAKEAWAY

As guests, we can play a more proactive role in rescuing restaurant experiences that are on the verge of failing. Certain variables will always be out of our control, but when we approach conflict more empathetically, it's easier to resolve common problems that might plague service. How we choose to communicate our needs and our grievances can weigh heavily in how a restaurant staff addresses them.

CHAPTER TEN

The Ins and Outs
of Tipping

Waiters are seldom socialists.

—GEORGE ORWELL

In over two decades waiting tables, I only questioned a bad tip once. I was serving a table of four businessmen from out of town who'd arrived for a late dinner. I patiently helped them navigate the menu, recommended dishes, and orchestrated a plan to suit their needs. By the end of their meal, they all seemed quite satisfied and were very complimentary of the food. When they requested the check, they asked me if I could help them play "credit card roulette." I'd seen this party trick before: everyone throws their credit cards into a pile, and someone is asked to randomly select one of the cards to pay the entire bill.

However, instead of simply placing the cards in the middle and asking me to select one, they asked me to summon the young, blonde hostess working at the door to do the honors. These men were all over fifty years old, each wearing a wedding ring. The hostess was a college student in her early twenties. I thought they were being creepy, but instead of acknowledging their creepiness, I tried to play it cool.

"Sorry, fellas, I'm the guy who brings food and drinks, not the guy who brings attractive women over to the table," I said, easing them down gently. When I returned, the men continued to press the issue, asking why the hostess hadn't visited the table yet. This time, I made it clear more firmly that I was uncomfortable with what they were asking me to do. After a while, they begrudgingly relented but clearly still felt miffed. Instead, they instructed me to split the bill evenly on the four cards. Each of the men abruptly signed the receipts before bolting for the exit. *Bad tippers always leave quickly.* All four men left zero tip on their $200 portions of the bill. Under normal circumstances, I would've received at least a $160 tip from a table with a similar check, assuming everyone was satisfied with their service, which until I spurned their game of credit card roulette, I thought these men were.

Despite having performed my job well and served their table with integrity, the simple fact that I wouldn't enlist a female coworker to boost their fragile male egos led them to unanimously decide to shortchange my tip. In doing so, they chose to cheat not only me but also the entire FOH team: the bartender who stirred their cocktails, the bussers who cleared their dirty plates, and the food runners who delivered their food from the kitchen. So, against my better judgment, I followed the four men out of the restaurant and confronted them on the sidewalk outside.

"Excuse me, gentlemen," I said, more politely than they deserved, "did you decide not to tip me because I wouldn't bring the hostess over to your table?" The men turned around, looking shocked that I had the nerve to question them.

"Actually, yes we did," said one of the men.

"Just so you know, I take a lot of pride in my work," I said, slowly measuring my words, "and I find it offensive that you think that part of my job is to serve you female attention." The men puffed up their chests but remained quiet. After a few tense moments, they scurried off into an Uber back to their bougie Midtown hotel.

I turned around and calmly walked back inside the restaurant. My manager wasn't pleased when I reported what I'd done and insisted that I should've let management handle the situation. If I wasn't a tenured member of the staff, I might've been fired on the spot. But to this day, I don't regret the decision to stick up for myself and my female colleague one bit.

This scenario demonstrates the power imbalances that make tipping so fraught. Entitled guests often withhold tips as a way to punish servers who aren't willing to bend the knee (as I wouldn't do for these men).

Since 1991, the federal minimum wage for tipped workers has been a paltry $2.13 per hour, versus the current $7.25 for non-tipped workers. Although many states have raised their tipped minimum wages, in most cases a server's income is determined more by the generosity of their guests than by the restaurant owners who employ them. This puts servers in a difficult predicament. They have a primary responsibility to the restaurant to do their jobs well, but they also need to show fidelity to the guests who are responsible for paying most of their salary. That quandary makes tolerating abuse and playing along with obnoxious behavior an inescapable hazard of the job.

In recent years, tipping culture in America has spiraled out of control, and the backlash among consumers has reached a fever pitch. It seems like whenever someone serves you these days—whether it's the barista who froths your latte, the bathroom attendant who offers you a paper towel in a swanky nightclub, or the guy in a jumpsuit pumping your gas—you're expected to leave a tip. Despite the backlash, however, Americans just can't seem to quit tipping. Restaurant owners have tried to find clever ways to add service charges to the bill or raise prices with service included, but most initiatives to abolish tipping have failed quite miserably.

Studies show that tipping is becoming increasingly unpopular among American consumers. According to a Bankrate survey in 2024, 59 percent of Americans viewed tipping negatively, and over a third of respondents believed that tipping culture has gotten out of control. But somehow the custom has remained resilient.

In my experience, most substandard tips aren't due to negative judgments about the service. They usually result from some combination of ignorance and ambivalence. Absent-minded people walk out of restaurants all the time forgetting to sign their credit card slips, which inadvertently deprives the server of any tip they'd intended to leave. Lousy tips come with the territory when you wait tables, so tipped workers develop thick skins and, for the most part, short memories. Anyone who can't shake off the ego-bruising effects of a bad tip won't last very long in the restaurant industry. Servers know that approaching guests who've under-tipped will rarely result in any kind of justice or recompense; it's much more likely to result in unemployment.

That's why it's considered heresy for waiters to question bad tips. But try to imagine a client underpaying for services in your line of work and your having to accept being shortchanged without a word of protest. Meanwhile, many restaurant guests, especially international tourists, are still confused about tipping rules. Other people fully understand the rules but choose to ignore them. Some guests are just cheap. But anyone who has ever worked in a restaurant will tell you, unequivocally, that a bad tip without probable cause is the ultimate form of disrespect. Waiters take it personally, and they *always* remember the worst offenders.

AN UNPOPULAR CUSTOM WITH A CHECKERED PAST

Modern tipping culture traces back to medieval Europe, when *vails* (small tokens of respect) were offered to servants for exceptional service. There is ongoing debate about the word's origin. One popular yet widely debunked origin story is that the term is an acronym for "To Insure Promptitude," allegedly coined in the 1760s. But the word appears to have been in regular usage among English servants a decade earlier. The common terms for tips in Germany and France at the time—*Trinkgeld* and *pourboire*, respectively—loosely translated mean "drinking money," a convivial, albeit patronizing, way to compensate a servant.

As tipping culture evolved across Europe, it became increasingly transactional. Elliott Shore and Katie Rawson noted in *Dining Out: A Global History of Restaurants:* "Tipping bubbles up to the surface the complicated dynamics of restaurants: having a relationship around food that is explicitly not commensal, which is defined by a market relationship." The practice of leaving gratuities appears to have been widely adopted in the United States after the Civil War and had become commonplace by the Roaring Twenties.

The Dark Side of Tipping

A landmark Cornell University study in 2008 that examined the effects of race, both of servers and customers, on tipping, led researchers to troubling conclusions about how racism influences tipping practices. The study revealed that both Black and white people regularly discriminated against Black servers by tipping them less. When respondents rated their service a perfect score, white servers' tips went up almost 7 percent, while the tipping percentage for Black servers remained the same (16.6 percent of the total bill), even when their service was also rated perfect. Beyond racial discrimination, similar studies have also shown problematic trends about gender bias in tipping. A 2014 report by Restaurant Opportunities Center United entitled *The Glass Floor* examined the link between tipping and sexual harassment among women in the restaurant industry. The study found that tipping systems in restaurants create a culture of sexual objectification, which disproportionally impacts women, with the highest rates of harassment occurring in states with the lowest hourly wages for tipped workers or places where female restaurant workers relied more on tips for income.

By the mid-nineteenth century, tipping had been embraced by large employers in the United States such as the Pullman Palace Car Company to artificially suppress wages for Black workers. By shifting the burden of paying their staff to their customers, tipping allowed many white-owned businesses at the time to control labor costs while also reinforcing power structures that oppressed Black workers.

But even while large companies legitimized the practice of tipping, the custom continued to have its critics, especially among organized labor. The writer William Scott excoriated the practice in his 1916 book, *The Itching Palm: A Study of the Habit of Tipping in America*, calling tipping, and the aristocratic idea it exemplifies, "a cancer on the breast of democracy." His principal argument is that tipping perpetuates nondemocratic class distinctions based on the exchange of money for servitude.

In the early 1900s, several states passed legislation to outlaw the practice, but those laws were abandoned by the time the federal government began regulating the minimum wage in 1938, which included provisions permitting employers to pay tipped workers a lower hourly rate.

Today the practice of tipping has become so commonplace that many American consumers are experiencing what has become known as "tipping fatigue." A study by Pew Research in 2023 found that 72 percent of respondents felt tipping was expected in more places than it had been five years earlier. Many consumers are exhausted by the constant bombardment of tip requests from Uber drivers, food delivery apps, maid services, and baristas. A landlord went viral on TikTok in 2023 after suggesting that tenants should add tips to their rent bill.

A TIP IS NOT A TAX

Since a gratuity is often paid as a percentage of the cost of a meal, skyrocketing menu prices have made tipping feel even more like an added tax, which it really isn't. In most full-service restaurants, tips constitute the lion's share of a staff's nightly earnings. Unfortunately, too many consumers still think of a tip as an evaluation of service, a token of appreciation, or simply "leaving extra." But the reality is that the substandard wages of tipped workers are subsidizing menu prices to keep them artificially low. In other words, if you choose not to leave a tip, then you are willfully enjoying a cheaper meal without properly compensating the staff for their service.

It's easy to fall into the trap of feeling animosity about tipping practices, instead of trying to understand how the system works, who benefits from it, and why. Studies have shown that younger consumers, Millennials and Gen Zers, are rejecting tipping and feel less inclined to follow established customs they had no hand in establishing. But understand that whether you support tipping or not, every time you dine out you are participating in a system that keeps restaurant meals priced artificially low because tipped workers are legally allowed to be paid subminimum wages. Even if you abhor the practice, a proper tip represents the cost of service, which in most restaurants is not included in the price of your meal.

A GENEROUS TIP
GETS PEOPLE'S ATTENTION

Putting aside its unsavory past, if deployed properly, tipping can be an effective tool for getting what you want in a restaurant. On the surface, it's still the most reliable way to show gratitude to your servers for a job well done. Some people work in restaurants because they genuinely love hospitality, but most restaurant professionals are there to make money. Earning a reputation as a consistently generous tipper is an effective way to get yourself noticed.

Across Europe—where tipping is virtually nonexistent—you rarely encounter as many motivated servers as you find in the United States. That's not to say that the American system is superior. Americans often characterize lackadaisical service pejoratively as "European style," to signify the more laid-back approach found throughout the European Union, where most member countries eschew tipping. In the United States, we expect our servers to hustle, and most American guests are willing to leave big tips for the ones who do.

On the surface, tipping creates a meritocracy that's consistent with many other commission-based industries in the United States—like real estate brokerages, stock trading firms, and talent agencies—in which pay is tied to performance. Whether we like it or not, tipping reflects our uniquely American values—as ugly as they may be at times—mirroring how free market capitalism influences almost every consumer behavior in our daily lives.

Despite the frustration it provokes among the masses, the tipping system still effectively ensures that a restaurant's front of house staff is personally invested in every guest's satisfaction because their income relates directly to their performance. Since tips are typically paid as a percentage of sales, making sure that every guest leaves satisfied is in the server's best interests economically. The downside is that the system also inherently discriminates against people who spend less (which is consistent with many other commercial transactions in which how much you spend dictates the service you receive, like flying first class in an airplane versus flying coach). But the upside is that guests can take advantage of the system by regularly rewarding staff with generous tips in service of building a reputation as a valued customer.

SHARING THE WEALTH

Most of the time when you leave a tip—especially in fine dining restaurants, where roles are more compartmentalized—it is shared among the staff. "Pooling" tips, meaning collecting servers' tips into a pool and dividing them according to a predetermined formula, is often essential to building solidarity among the FOH staff. While some servers prefer to reap only what they sow, most staff learn to appreciate pooling because it insulates them against the risk of bad tips and spreads the wealth when there are generous ones. In a pooled house, a rising tide lifts all boats. Pooling tips guarantees that nobody's boat is bigger than anyone else's. It also prevents anyone's boat from sinking, and most importantly, it ensures that the crew doesn't start throwing each other overboard.

While tip pooling fosters a deeper sense of shared responsibility among the staff, the system also has plenty of shortcomings. Sharing tips can lead to discord over whether everyone on staff is pulling their weight. When tips are shared, staff members who are perceived to be slackers will be accused of "surfing the pool" (meaning they're riding on everyone else's coattails), which can cause rifts and disrupt unity.

But by mitigating boom or bust nights for individual servers, pooling tips provides income stability for FOH staff. Servers in non-pooled houses may be more motivated, but service can suffer when they are only focused on the guests in their section and ignore everyone else. However, even where tips aren't pooled, waiters in most restaurants are still expected to "tip out" a portion of their earnings to support staff like bussers and food runners (usually a fixed percentage of their total tips).

Regardless of whether a staff pools tips or not, hospitality standards are difficult to maintain without the feeling of common purpose that pooling tips can help engender.

HOW MUCH SHOULD YOU TIP?

At the very least, a generous tip demonstrates that you value the selflessness and sacrifice that goes into delivering attentive service. But the psychology behind tipping can be much more complicated. Some psychologists see it as a form of ego boost for the person issuing the tip; studies suggest that generous tippers may be looking for acceptance or social approval. Tipping can also be a way to allay anxiety or insecurity. Anecdotally, I've noticed that many customers whose credit cards get declined often overcompensate by leaving oversized tips, perhaps to avoid being perceived by the server (or their dining companions) as financially insecure.

Experienced servers can often tell immediately whether someone is a generous tipper or not. Good tippers tend to be more gregarious toward their servers; bad tippers tend to be more standoffish and withdrawn. Waiters joke privately about a phenomenon they call the "verbal tip"—when a guest is thrilled with service, thanks the server profusely on the way out, but then leaves an insufficient tip. It's always nice to be complimented when a guest leaves satisfied, but kind words don't pay the rent.

There is still a great deal of confusion about tipping. A third of respondents in the 2023 Pew Research study reported feeling confused about knowing whether they should tip or how much they should tip in different hospitality settings. In fine dining restaurants, the 15 percent tip, long considered the gold standard for exceptional service, is now considered an average tip (the Pew study found that 57 percent of Americans still tip 15 percent or less in most situations). By today's standards, diners should tip at least 18 to 20 percent of the total bill if service is excellent. When it surpasses expectations, guests can exceed that amount at their own discretion. If the kitchen sends complimentary items to your table, as they might when you visit a friend who works in a restaurant, you should consider the value of those complimentary items when determining the tip amount.

SHOULD I TIP ON THE WINE?

The question of whether you should include the cost of alcohol or wine in calculating the tip is one of the most controversial issues surrounding tipping. Detractors will say, "All the server did was remove the cork from the bottle and pour it, so why should I have to leave them so much extra money just for that?" Those who support tipping on wine will argue that staff often provides invaluable expertise that makes the wine service an integral part of the experience. While both arguments have merit, remember that tipping generously on big-ticket items like luxury wines may not only affect your current experience, but it may also potentially affect your future ones.

If a businessperson frequently hosts clients in an upscale restaurant and is attended to closely by the wine staff, for example, it's in the guest's best interest to tip generously on the cost of the wine. Over time, the staff will recognize their generosity and, hopefully, go the extra mile to provide more personalized attention. This might include decanting older wines ahead of time, procuring special selections that aren't offered to the public, or pouring a complimentary digestif to end the meal. If the guest chooses not to tip on the wine or tips at a lower percentage rate than they do on the food portion of the bill, staff may harbor resentment, which could jeopardize the quality of their service going forward.

When it comes to recommending wine or wine pairings, most sommeliers take pride in offering thoughtful recommendations or taking time to share their knowledge with guests. Being on the receiving end of this kind of personalized wine service justifies augmenting the tip. If you choose a five-hundred-dollar bottle of Bordeaux without having any conversation with the staff at all, then you may feel less inclined to tip on the price of the bottle. But keep in mind that even when they don't help you choose wine, sommeliers still provide comprehensive service beyond simply offering recommendations: decanting delicate bottles, checking the wine for flaws, and keeping your glasses full throughout the meal.

NEVER USE A TIP AS A PUNISHMENT

When guests leave without tipping for service, waiters call it "stiffing." Stiffing a waiter is *never* justified, except in isolated cases in which a staff member was abusive or put guests in harm's way. It's important to understand that when you're leaving a substandard tip, it penalizes the entire staff, not just the person you perceive to be at fault for the deficiencies in service. If the food runners brought your food to the table without incident and bussers kept your table well manicured throughout the meal, there's no reason that those staff members should suffer because you had bad chemistry with the waiter.

I once had a table leave me a 10 percent tip after showing no signs of being unhappy with my service. A week later, I discovered a negative Yelp review that described my service as negligent. The guest accused me of spending all my time "flirting with the pretty girls" at the bar. The "pretty girls" were my aunt and her friend, who'd come in to have a drink and say hello. I was not flirting at all, nor do I think that I was being inattentive toward this table. The guest had simply invented a narrative to justify punishing me with a bad tip. This is not uncommon, especially when guests find themselves in unpleasant situations like a bad date, a lover's quarrel, or an argument with a parent. These guests often scapegoat the staff, even though the staff isn't to blame for whatever unpleasantness caused their misery.

If you're disappointed with service, it's always more productive to contact the restaurant the next day to speak with management about your issue rather than leaving a deficient tip. When handled constructively, these conversations can be great learning experiences for staff. But they can also be illuminating for the guest who feels aggrieved. They may learn subsequently that the service delays were caused by malfunctioning kitchen equipment or a surprise visit from the health depart-

Where Does My Tip Go?

When you tip a server fifty dollars, the fifty dollars doesn't go directly into their pocket. In fact, most of the time, the server only takes home a fraction of the total because tips are often shared among the entire FOH team. In most full-service restaurants, there is a platoon of bussers and food runners who are paid from the tip pool. The bar team also receives a share, including a barback who keeps the bar stocked with ice and supplies throughout the night. Depending on the circumstances, maître d's or hosts may also be paid fractionally from the tip pool. In fine dining restaurants, if a sommelier assists with wine service, they will also get tipped out. So, let's consider that fifty-dollar tip you left. Depending on how the tip pool is disseminated, ten dollars may be divided among the bussers and another ten dollars among the food runners. The bartender and sommelier will also take five dollars each. If the maître d' or host also takes a cut, the waiter will end up pocketing less than half of the original tip. The more staff that is needed to maintain proper standards, the smaller the pieces of the pie become. Finding the right balance of staffing levels that also provides suitable tip income to FOH staff can be a complicated formula, especially for new restaurants.

ment, not lazy or incompetent staff. At the end of the day, leaving a bad tip doesn't teach anyone any lessons. It's just flat-out mean.

A TIP IS A REWARD, NOT A BRIBE

Slipping the maître d' a cash bribe in exchange for a nice table is an old-school mafioso move, but trying to buy your way into a trendy restaurant these days can be tricky. "Greasing the door," as we used to call it, was much more common decades ago than it is now. Most maître d's in high-end restaurants today are careful not to broker too many deals with the devil. Nevertheless, contrary to public perception, restaurants aren't democracies; everyone doesn't always have an equal chance of getting a table. In fact, most upscale restaurants operate much more like meritocracies. Big spenders tend to have a much easier time getting a reservation.

If you attempt to buy your way into a restaurant, you should always be prepared for a doorperson to accept your tip without delivering results right away. Any time money changes hands like this in a restaurant, you are investing in a partnership that can take time to develop. Nurturing those relationships over time by tipping generously or offering other nonmonetary compensation like free concert tickets is a much more effective way to convince a maître d' you're worth being taken care of than a one-off bribe.

In my opinion, the best way to curry favor with restaurant gatekeepers is to tip them on the way out. Obviously, this doesn't help in circumstances when you urgently need a table and don't have one reserved, but it's a much more effective way to show your appreciation to the person who oversees the reservation book. It also increases the chances they'll remember you the next time you need a booking. If you don't have any cash on you, drop off a card the next day with a crisp fifty-dollar bill for the maître d', manager, or reservationist who helped you book the table. Even at the toughest doors in the city, being consistently generous to the gatekeeper will make it harder and harder for them to say no when you need a table.

HANDSHAKE TIPS ARE AWKWARD

Maybe the handshake tip was glamorous back in the day, when high rollers would walk into restaurants with wads of hundred-dollar bills, but glad-handing staff in exchange for preferential treatment, especially when the bills are smaller than hundreds, has fallen out of favor in restaurants these days. In some cases, handing out cash can be an effective way to send a message to the server: "You scratch my back, I'll scratch yours." But it can also come across as demeaning and gross.

In the restaurant business, we refer to handshake tips as "palming." The people doing the palming are usually more impressed with themselves for making the gesture than the people who receive it are with someone trying to buy their affection. And while an unexpected bonus can be a nice surprise for the server, in my experience people who leave palm tips also expect that they're purchasing loyalty with it. Waiters have an entire section to manage, so being expected to show fealty to someone who paid for their allegiance can be a risky proposition.

If you insist on palming your server, do it discreetly once you've established a rapport. Ideally approach them away from the table, hand them the cash without making a show of concealing it, and tell them how much you appreciate their service. A creepy handshake with hidden funds makes the transaction feel somehow forbidden or illegitimate, like squaring up with a sex worker. A more graceful way of delivering a palm tip is to ask for an empty check presenter, place the cash inside, and hand the concealed cash directly to the recipient.

CHECK YOUR MATH AND MAKE SURE
TO LEAVE A SIGNATURE

You'd be shocked at how many diners forget to sign their credit card receipt. It happens all the time, and it drives servers crazy. Most of the time when this happens, guests sign both copies of the receipt and forget to leave one on the table. I've even had parties walk out of the restaurant without paying their check completely because everyone thought someone else at the table had already paid. It is not fun as a waiter when you have to stop everything and chase a table down the street because they forgot to pay or neglected to leave behind a signed copy of the receipt.

Leaving a signed credit card slip is important for many reasons. First, the server cannot receive whatever tip you intended to leave without it. It's soul crushing to servers when they gave their heart and soul to take care of a table that left happy, then have to close their check without any tip because the guest forgot to leave a signed copy of the receipt. Second, a signed credit card receipt is required to verify all credit card transactions; most restaurants keep a signed copy of every credit card sale on file in case any charges are disputed. But in most cases, as long as the credit card has been authorized successfully, restaurants will allow the check to be settled without a signature. In other words, the restaurant will get its money, but, assuming the customer intended to leave a tip, the server will get nothing.

Whenever you're splitting the bill on multiple credit cards, make sure that everyone understands their share of the tip amount and fills out their credit card slips accordingly. Too often in my experience, splitting the bill according to some complex mathematical equation causes confusion that usually ends up shortchanging the server. No matter how many drinks you've had or how much euphoria you may be feeling after a satisfying meal, always take a few extra seconds before you leave to make sure you've filled out the tip amount legibly and left a signed copy of the check behind for the server. It doesn't hurt to double-check your math, too, to make sure you've correctly totaled the bill. If you don't, your server may be left guessing about how much tip you intended to leave, which could lead to your being overcharged.

WHY TIPPING MATTERS

On a very chaotic night of service, a fellow server once approached me in a panic to ask a favor. He was taking care of a regular guest who he knew was a huge tipper. About ten minutes earlier, we'd sold out of duck fat potatoes, one of our most popular side dishes, and the big tipper's table really wanted them. My colleague went back to the kitchen and saw that guests at a table in my section who'd ordered the potatoes hadn't received their entrées yet. "Is there any way we can give yours to this guy? He always leaves us crisp hundreds in cash," said my coworker.

Essentially, my colleague was asking me to lie and tell my table, who'd ordered the potatoes at least a half-hour earlier, that suddenly we didn't have an order for them. We pooled our tips in this restaurant, so a big cash tip from my coworker's table would benefit me too. Before approaching my table, I weighed the potential backlash. They seemed like they were having a great time, and we'd built a solid rapport. I told my colleague that I would see what I could do.

I sauntered over to my table with a somber expression and politely interrupted their conversion. "I'm terribly sorry, guys," I said. "It turns out we don't have an order of the duck fat potatoes for your table, so the chef is going to send out some grilled oyster mushrooms and purple asparagus instead with our compliments." They accepted the news charitably and even seemed excited about the extras. I went back to my colleague and told him he could have his table's potatoes. I sent the couple at my table an extra dessert on top of the free side dishes, and they left smiling. It wasn't my proudest moment, but nobody got hurt, and the generous tipper left us two hundred dollars in cash on a five-hundred-dollar check (a 40 percent tip).

I'm sure there are far less nefarious examples of how tipping well encourages servers to go the extra mile. But the important point to make here is that if you take care of the staff regularly, they will take care of you. Restaurant workers always remember generous guests, and they will fight harder for those people. Try not to think of your tip only as rewarding the staff for attentive service today. It can also be a way to strengthen your reputation over the long term.

THE TAKEAWAY

Tipping customs in America are deeply flawed and rooted in racism and misogyny. But while tipping historically promulgates systematic inequities, it's also likely not going away anytime soon. Being a mindful and generous tipper is still the most effective way to show gratitude for hospitable service. Servers pay attention to who tips well, and having a consistent record of generosity is the most reliable way to earn preferred status.

CHAPTER ELEVEN

How to Become a Regular

It's easier to be faithful to a restaurant than
it is to be faithful to a woman.

—FEDERICO FELLINI

When the COVID-19 pandemic hit in March 2020, the restaurant where I was working abruptly closed. The entire staff, over one hundred employees, were laid off overnight. None of us had ever experienced anything like it. The restaurant industry has always been a dependable source of employment for millions of people, and a world without fancy places to dine was a contingency that none of us had ever considered. A few days later, the staff received an email from management explaining that a wealthy regular of the restaurant had made a twenty-thousand-dollar donation to help the staff through the period of closure. We were stunned. The fact that someone cared so deeply about our welfare simply because they had dined in our restaurant regularly was one of the most touching gestures I've ever experienced in my restaurant career.

Obviously, not every restaurant regular can make a cash donation of this magnitude, but humble gestures can often be just as meaningful. Arriving with a box of homemade chocolate chip cookies or a bag of souvenir trinkets from a recent vacation can be touching ways to show the staff that you appreciate them. In hospitality, we spend so much energy making other people feel special that it can be very moving when guests turn the hospitality on us.

Beloved regulars become adopted into our restaurant families. We often bestow honorifics upon them that conjure familial acceptance like "Uncle Jimmy" or "Mama O." They understand that with the privilege of being a restaurant regular comes great responsibility. If service is slow one night or the food isn't as consistent as usual, regulars will always be more willing to forgive. They show up during snowstorms and natural disasters. They close ranks when someone in the restaurant family is injured or struggling and are always there to lend a hand during times of crisis, as many regulars did during the pandemic.

The most exclusive restaurants in the world—including ones with months-long waiting lists such as Eleven Madison Park in New York City or Noma in Copenhagen—have regular guests. While it's true that regulars at elite restaurants often cultivate preferred status by spending exorbitant sums of money, many of them also earn it by being dependable guests who treat the staff kindly. It takes time and commitment, but one of the best strategies for consistently getting into a busy restaurant is to become a familiar face by dining there more frequently. Even the trendiest restaurants will give preferential treatment to their most loyal patrons.

When a restaurant is hard to get into, earning regular status can be challenging. But it is never impossible. It usually comes down to perseverance. Unfortunately, average diners get discouraged easily when they can't get an 8:00 p.m. reservation on a Saturday night. They don't always have the tenacity to keep trying when a restaurant is consistently fully booked. But regulars always keep trying. They call the same day to check if there are any cancellations. They show up unannounced in case a table might have opened up at the last minute.

I've worked in a handful of New York City hotspots through the years, restaurants that everyone would swear were *impossible* to get into, and I would always see familiar faces every night. Most of those regulars had fostered personal relationships with the staff over time that helped facilitate access. Management will never admit to playing favorites, but when it's in the restaurant's best interest to show favor to valued regular guests, they will. But cracking the code is a complex process. A true regular has a deeper, more intimate relationship with the restaurant and its staff than others, one that can only be earned through consistent, unwavering patronage.

Most restaurants don't have an unlisted phone number for VIPs or a secret email address for reservations, no matter how much you badger the poor reservationist about it. Your inability to procure a prime-time reservation usually comes down to supply and demand. If you really want to become a regular at a restaurant badly enough, the most effective shortcut is to get to know the people who work there. But it takes more than one visit to develop that connection.

Unfortunately, we live in world of instant gratification, in which diners expect everything right away without a need for personal sacrifice beyond the cost of the meal. Most people would rather complain about how hard it is to get into a popular restaurant than to show up at 5:30 p.m. on a Tuesday in the dead of winter to see if a walk-in table is available. Even though most reservations are made digitally these days, restaurants are still much easier to hack through analog means, by forging meaningful relationships with the people who run them.

PROVING YOUR WORTH

Excessive spending isn't the only reliable way of becoming a regular. In most cases, simply being consistently gracious and considerate of the staff can take you just as far. Restaurant workers are accustomed to being treated like "the help," so when guests make a genuine effort to get to know them, it can go a long way toward establishing a mutually beneficial relationship. It's important to let this relationship develop on the restaurant's terms, though. The staff can be suspicious of guests who cozy up to them too quickly looking for an advantage. The strategy will backfire if team members think you're only being friendly because you need help getting a reservation.

Think of becoming a regular like starting a romantic relationship. You can't force a prospective partner to be committed right away; the chemistry needs to build organically. If you come on too strong, it might push the person away. When you meet someone new, there is always a feeling-out period. At that point, you might be mutually attracted, but it's way too early to start thinking about making a commitment. By the third or fourth date, if you both still like each other, then you start clearing your schedule to prioritize the relationship. But it's unreasonable to expect a new romantic partner to be exclusive when you've just met and haven't yet proven yourself to be a worthy companion. It's the same in restaurants—recognition must be earned by proving your worth and developing a reliable track record. If you only pick up the phone to call occasionally and aren't consistently interested, then both romantic partners and restaurants probably won't think you're serious about taking the relationship to the next level.

ENJOYING THE CREATURE COMFORTS

I was having a conversation with a friend recently about how chain restaurants like Applebee's and Olive Garden are engineered for consistency. Loyal fans gravitate toward these brands because they know that the dining experience will be virtually identical across every location. Predictability is integral to their appeal. My friend told me about how her grandfather meets with a group of retired friends every Monday morning to have coffee at the local Burger King in town to chat about current events and politics. They never order any food. They have a regular table where they just sit and chat with their coffees, and they never miss a week.

Restaurant regulars are creatures of habit. Many of them order the same food every time. They make special requests for the chef to prepare their favorite dish a certain way—sauce on the side, light on the salt, simply steamed with olive oil. I've worked in restaurants that went so far as naming new dishes on the menu after regulars when a frequent guest ordered a customized dish so often that it became a permanent fixture. Regulars order the same cocktail every time, prepared the same way by the same bartender—extra dirty martini, splash of vermouth, reserve the dirty rocks on the side. If they don't like the way the other bartender makes it, they only come in on the nights that their guy's behind the bar.

When they're having dinner, they sit at the very same table every time, sometimes in the very same chair.

Patience Is a Virtue

A dedicated regular will always be more willing to wait for a table than others. From the restaurant's perspective, someone who will patiently stand by for a walk-in table or be willing to endure protracted seating delays is worth their weight in gold. Here's why: when restaurants have last-minute cancellations or no-shows, having loyal regulars walk in unannounced, happy to have a drink at the bar and wait until a table becomes available, helps replenish lost revenue. But even when regulars have a reservation, they tend to be more understanding about being seated late compared with average guests who are easily irritated by a fifteen-minute wait. Seating every guest on time is one of the biggest challenges that restaurants face every day. If your table isn't available at your scheduled reservation time, have a drink at the bar. If it ends up being a longer wait, order another round. If the wait becomes intolerable, ask if you can pre-order your food so that it will be ready once you sit down. More than any other attribute, patience is essential to becoming a restaurant regular.

There's a primal comfort in the familiarity of a disciplined restaurant that recognizes regulars. Restaurateurs like Danny Meyer, of Union Square Hospitality Group, have built empires around the art of anticipating guests' needs and customizing service in a way that makes diners feel seen. In Meyer's restaurants, the staff is trained to make notes on each diner's digital profile with detailed information about their eating and drinking habits. These notes are passed along to every server and bartender whenever a regular guest comes in to dine at any of the company's restaurants. This way frequent visitors don't need to share the specs on their martini or explain their food allergies every time—the bartender or server already knows what they prefer the moment they sit down. When you find a restaurant that understands you in this way, you never feel the need to go anywhere else.

But enjoying preferred status does not mean that regulars should feel entitled to special treatment. If their food isn't quite as good as usual, they should always be willing to share constructive criticism, never petty complaints. If the chef sends out complimentary dishes to acknowledge their continued patronage, regulars should be gracious and thank them—but never expect freebies on future visits. They should always tip generously, even when service isn't at its finest. Becoming a restaurant regular is about more than just visiting a restaurant consistently. Regulars are fiercely loyal, and they always stay humble.

SHOW INTEREST IN THE STAFF
WITHOUT BEING INTRUSIVE

If you feel a connection with a staff member, it's better to wait until you've established a rapport before asking their name or other personal questions. Start by showing genuine interest in what they do in the restaurant, instead of asking about their lives outside of work. Most restaurant workers love sharing their expertise about food and wine with guests who appreciate the breadth of their knowledge. Before peppering your server with personal questions that they may be uncomfortable answering, engage them in conversation about the menu and ask for recommendations. Once you've established a more organic connection, then it's appropriate to introduce yourself and ask for their name.

Avoid questions that pry into their personal lives like "Where did you grow up?" or "How long have you lived in the city?" Answering seemingly harmless questions like "What other restaurants have you worked in before this one?" can be uncomfortable for some restaurant workers, who would rather not divulge their work history (which could be complicated) to complete strangers. If a staff member wants to share personal information with you, let them do so on their own schedule.

As much as you may feel a kinship with someone serving you, I don't recommend ever making overtures about extending a relationship with a staff member outside of work (such as asking your server to join you and your friends for drinks after their shift). If an opportunity arises to exchange personal information, ideally, it should be initiated by the staff member, not the guest. When guests solicit staff about making plans outside of work, it puts the staff in an uncomfortable position, especially in cases when they aren't interested in pursuing a relationship beyond the professional variety.

ALWAYS BE ON YOUR BEST BEHAVIOR

It goes without saying that the best restaurant regulars are also the most consistently well behaved. But what makes these guests so unique and special is their sincerity. They are consistently gracious and polite but also predictable. Having the discipline to consistently be on your best behavior is essential to earning regular status. A frequent guest can be the nicest person four out of five visits, but if they come in drunk and belligerent one time, it violates the trust that is essential to becoming a regular.

Great regulars adapt to the surroundings and go with the flow. They blend in with the scenery like houseplants. A cherished regular never rests on their laurels; they maintain their reputation by showing up when others don't and consistently being one less thing for the staff to worry about. The most valued regulars understand and accept that every restaurant is a product of years of knowledge and expertise. They never try to project their own image of what they think a restaurant should be. They accept the restaurant for what it is.

LOYALTY IS EVERYTHING

No one should expect special treatment if they only visit a restaurant sporadically. A romantic relationship would never take the next step if a couple only made plans once every few months. Restaurant relationships are no different. Loyal patronage is critical to a restaurant's longevity, and smart business owners value their most loyal guests above casual customers. They remember and reward people who have supported them consistently over the years.

At one place I worked, which was almost impossible to get into, we had a regular guest with a standing reservation every Monday night at 8:00 p.m. In the three-year period since the restaurant had been open, he'd already logged in over a hundred visits. The guy wasn't a particularly extravagant spender, but he always received preferential treatment because he brought in more business by introducing the restaurant to colleagues and friends, who subsequently became clients themselves. Some regulars are more loyal to their favorite restaurants than they are to their spouses. We know because they often come in with their lovers.

BECOME A BRAND AMBASSADOR

Good old-fashioned word of mouth is still the most effective grassroots advertising for any restaurant business. Regulars don't just routinely dine in a restaurant; they also become evangelists for the place. There's an old saying that a person will tell one friend about a great restaurant experience, but they'll tell ten people about a bad one. Restaurants rely on regulars to act as enthusiastic ambassadors for their brand who spread positive word of mouth and help bring new customers into the fold.

Management notices when regulars share their love of the restaurant with friends and family. Those friends often become regulars themselves, and they bring in other friends. One regular can create a virtuous cycle that single-handedly keeps a restaurant's seats full over time. The regular who sits at the bar alone every Friday night is appreciated, but the one who is committed to spreading the gospel to others is priceless.

MEMBERSHIP HAS ITS PRIVILEGES

These days, exclusive members-only restaurants are popping up in big cities like New York; their annual dues can be up to $100,000 a year.

It's hard to imagine anyone paying that much money for the privilege of private dining, but the feeling of belonging that comes with being a restaurant regular can be intoxicating.

The same feeling can apply to participating in restaurant rewards programs, common among many chain brands such as TGI Fridays and Red Lobster that reward consistent patronage by offering special perks like free appetizers or collectible merchandise for repeat guests. These loyalty programs are designed to reinforce consumer habits, but they're also meant to make regulars feel special by offering exclusive discounts or limited-time-only promotions.

Once you've become a regular in your favorite restaurant, there are many other peripheral benefits. Receiving special accommodation from the staff can pay dividends if you're looking to impress a date, consummate a business deal, or even strike up a friendship across the bar over a few martinis. Developing a deeper relationship with a restaurant also means that they should better understand how to serve your needs. Staff members can customize recommendations based on their familiarity with your personal preferences. If a nightly special is about to sell out early and they know you have a dinner reservation later, a staff member might reserve an order for you to make sure you don't miss the opportunity to try something new. Restaurants will always go out of their way to look out for their most valued regulars.

THE TAKEAWAY

Being a restaurant regular carries enormous responsibility, like marrying into a new family. Mindful guests never take that responsibility lightly. You can't become a restaurant regular overnight. It must be earned through consistent patronage and unwavering loyalty. Earning regular status should never be an excuse for complacency. The best regulars treat every visit as an opportunity to deepen their relationship with their favorite restaurants.

CHAPTER TWELVE

Tricks of the Trade, Power Moves, and No-No's

Look at your waiter's face. He knows.
It's another reason to be polite to your waiter:
he could save your life with a raised eyebrow or a sigh.

—ANTHONY BOURDAIN

In his book *Kitchen Confidential*, the legendary chef and author Anthony Bourdain shared candid insider secrets he had gleaned over decades working in professional kitchens. He warned us to avoid fish on Mondays (because there are no seafood deliveries on Sundays, and Monday's product is usually days old), to skip the special all-you-can-eat moules-frites (mussels are often poorly stored, and the chef puts them on special to get rid of them), and to never order anything with Hollandaise sauce during brunch (the egg yolk–based sauce, which needs to be tempered, is a breeding ground for bacteria). Bourdain is still revered by so many, and his legend lives on, because he was relentless in his commitment to sharing the truth about what happens behind the scenes in a restaurant.

When I worked in restaurants, especially in tourist destinations, guests would regularly ask me for recommendations about my favorite places to dine and drink. They were wise to ask. Most people who work in restaurants have their fingers on the pulse of the local dining scene. Not only will they tell you which local bar makes the greatest Negroni, but they'll also give you the name of the bartender who makes it, so you know who to ask for next time you walk in. As hospitality professionals, we spend so much time in restaurants that we become arbiters of good taste. Restaurants are our natural habitat.

When restaurant workers dine out, we hold ourselves to a high standard as guests because we know how we like to be treated when we serve others. If staff from other restaurants come in to dine where we work, we "style them out" with extras—complimentary wine pairings, desserts, or after-dinner drinks. The restaurant industry is a secret society in which membership is earned through long hours and a lot of blood, sweat, and tears. We understand the rigors of hospitality work, so we always want to make our extended industry family feel special, showering them with love every chance we get. And we can be sure they'll pay it forward when we visit their restaurants.

The average diner can learn a lot from how restaurant workers dine. If you were planning to start a business, you'd seek out a reputable accountant or tax professional to advise you. When it comes to dining better, restaurant workers know all the shortcuts and secret handshakes. They can also help you avoid common pitfalls, things that fluent restaurant guests should *never* do. Here are some nifty tricks, baller moves, dining hacks, and caveats that can help you on your way to becoming someone who dines like the pros do.

TRICKS OF THE TRADE

When you work in a restaurant, you always know when you're serving someone who has a restaurant background. They engage differently. They listen well and ask targeted questions. Sometimes the tells are very subtle, like when they ask, "Is the salmon wild or farm raised?" or "Do you have any Bordeaux producers from the Right Bank?" Restaurant workers know how much more flavorful wild salmon is than farmed and that the Right Bank of Bordeaux specializes in Merlot-based reds. Inexperienced restaurant guests can benefit from learning more tricks of the trade that will help them make the most out of their dining experiences. Here are a few ideas.

Wait a Few Months before Visiting a New Restaurant

Restaurants are like newborns. They need time to grow and mature. Newborn babies can't walk until they learn to crawl. Sometimes they spit up on you. Don't rush to be the first person to try a restaurant the minute it opens. Especially in the digital age, people feel the need to break the seal of a buzzed-about place for social media clout or to impress their followers, but new restaurants can be mistake prone in the early going. Give them time to find their footing, to refine their systems, and for the kitchen to develop more consistency with the menu. Also, the hype can be deafening in the first few months when a new place opens, so it pays to wait for the euphoria to subside a little.

Allow the Waiter to Plan Your Meal

If your server is knowledgeable about the menu and you've developed a good rapport, ask them to order your meal for you. It sends a strong message that you trust yourself in their care. Professional chefs do this at each others' restaurants all the time. They simply say, "Please ask the chef to cook for me!" Most servers love ordering for their tables; it's a fun challenge that breaks the monotony of rote order taking. You may not love every one of their choices, but you'll certainly end up with a more interesting meal and will get to try certain dishes that you never would've otherwise ordered. Showing faith in the staff builds solidarity too. When you allow a waiter to plan your menu, they become more personally invested in your dining experience.

Communicate Your Time Constraints When You Sit Down

When I waited tables, it amazed me how often people would wait until they were halfway through their meal to alert me that they had theater plans, concert tickets, or some other prior engagement. If you need to leave by a particular time, let your server know when you place the order or, even better, the moment you sit down. This information is vital to keeping your table on schedule. In some cases, your server may need to arrange with the chef to prioritize your table's order to ensure that the food comes out in a timely manner. It's impossible for the server to make these adjustments if you keep them in the dark about your schedule.

Offer the Server a Taste of Your Bottle of Wine

In restaurants that have massive wine lists, most servers don't have the opportunity to taste every selection, especially the most expensive bottles. Offering the waiter a taste of your wine is a thoughtful way to acknowledge their service. If your relationship is congenial, politely ask them if they've ever tasted the bottle you ordered. If they haven't, invite them to grab a glass for a taste. Pour the wine for them yourself, so they don't feel uncomfortable about how much of it to take. Some managers, especially in fine dining restaurants, might frown upon the idea of servers drinking alcohol in the dining room, but most establishments welcome it when it's for educational purposes. If you're knowledgeable about the wine you picked, share that knowledge with the server, but try not to present the information in a pedantic or condescending way.

Ask for the Manager to Give Praise

The phrase "May I speak to the manager?" is rarely followed by good tidings. Indeed, positive reinforcement does not come easily in the restaurant business. The loudest voices in the room are usually the unhappiest ones. Managers are accustomed to putting out fires and fielding complaints, but they *love* to chat with satisfied customers. So, the next time you're having a blast at a restaurant and you think the food and service is fantastic, ask to speak with the manager to give praise. It might cause the staff to panic momentarily as they brace for a Karen moment, but they'll be pleasantly surprised once they know your feedback is positive.

Order Birthday Desserts in Advance

Chain restaurants like Applebee's raised the bar for the industry (or lowered it, depending on where you work) when they started giving away free desserts to people celebrating birthdays. Nowadays, many diners feel entitled to a free dessert on their birthday, and pretty much everyone expects a chorus of servers to serenade their table with the Happy Birthday song. But the truth is most restaurants would go out of business if they gave away free desserts to every guest celebrating a birthday. If you'd like the restaurant to put a candle in someone's dessert, make a note of it on your reservation. Servers can often be confused about whose birthday it is at the table, so if you can, discreetly identify the guest of honor. If the birthday boy or girl doesn't care for dessert but you still want to celebrate, order something for the table and let the server know privately that you'd like them to add a candle. A great way to circumvent this problem is to order a dessert in advance—something simple like a slice of chocolate cake or a bowl of vanilla ice cream. This way, the restaurant can simply send out the preordered dessert with a candle as soon as the table is finished their savory courses.

POWER MOVES

Restaurant workers are not easily impressed. But there are ways to flaunt your dining acumen that will earn their respect. Most of these flexes are about demonstrating that you have deep respect for the staff and trust them implicitly to guide the way. Deferring to their expertise, by doing things like letting them select your bottle of wine for you, is the ultimate power move.

Make an Offering to the Kitchen

It's an unspoken tradition in many restaurants that when an employee comes in to have dinner, they bring beers (or other treats) for the kitchen. It's a thoughtful way to acknowledge the hardworking, and often underpaid, cooks who make the food taste so delicious. Back-of-the-house jobs can be thankless. Cooks often spend ten hours or more slaving away in a hot kitchen without breaks, and they appreciate it when guests acknowledge their work. An ice-cold beer at the end of an arduous shift can be nirvana for an exhausted line cook, but of course, a six-pack is not the only way to show appreciation. Stop by one of your favorite bakeries on the way to the restaurant and pick up an assortment of cookies. I'd recommend making your offering to the kitchen when you first arrive because the chef may want to reciprocate by sending a few extras to your table with the kitchen's compliments to say thanks.

Tip the Bussers When You Sit Down

As I mentioned when discussing tipping, giving discreet cash tips to staff can be awkward, and I really don't recommend the practice. But if you're going to invest in a member of the staff, in my opinion, bussers give you the best bang for your buck. First, they rarely receive tips directly from customers, so they appreciate it even more when it happens. Second, it can be an effective way to motivate them to maintain your table more fastidiously. Next thing you know, your bread basket is replenished without your asking, your water glasses are magically refilled every few minutes, and your table is cleared immediately as soon as you're done with each course. Support staff often spend more time attending to your table's needs directly than your waiter does, so tipping them is a worthwhile investment.

Ask the Sommelier to Choose Your Bottle of Wine

Instead of struggling to choose a bottle of wine or relying on the dubious trick of picking the second-most expensive bottle on the list, give the sommelier or server price parameters and ask them to pick a bottle for you. Most wine professionals revel in the opportunity to introduce someone to unfamiliar grapes, obscure wine-making regions, and sustainable producers. The wine universe is vast and can be intimidating for guests whose knowledge is limited. Asking the staff to choose your bottle not only takes the guesswork out of selecting wine, but it also makes the process more personalized and less transactional.

Nose the Wine, Don't Taste It

According to research by the National Institutes of Health, the human olfactory system can identify more than a trillion different scents. Your palate, on the other hand, can only detect five basic tastes: salt, sweet, bitter, sour, and umami. So, when the server presents your bottle of wine and offers you a splash, you may swirl and smell it, but you don't need to taste it immediately. As long as you don't detect any off-putting aromas, like wet newspaper or stewed fruit, then sampling the wine needn't be part of your evaluation. Of course, not everyone's sense of smell is equally refined, so if you don't trust your nasal prowess, that's fine. But one's sense of smell is still the most powerful tool they have for evaluating whether a wine is sound or not. As a bonus, the server or sommelier will be duly impressed when you ask them to pour the wine without taking a sip.

Send a Thank-You Note in the Mail

If you have an amazing restaurant experience, drop an old-school thank-you note in the snail mail. Restaurant workers don't receive much praise, so a handwritten note can be very touching. Sharing your appreciation in writing can also provide a nice jolt of positive reinforcement to boost the team's morale. When managers receive effusive thank-you notes from guests, they'll often share them publicly with the entire staff. In general, guests tend to be much more demonstrative when an experience disappoints, so offering commendation to counterbalance all the negativity really helps.

Bring Gifts during the Holidays

The holidays can be a very challenging time to work in a restaurant. Not only are you spending extended time away from your family and loved ones, but your work life becomes more fraught, as the pressure to create special holiday memories intensifies. Taking care of people dining with their families, especially the dysfunctional ones, can be exhausting. It's always a breath of fresh air during the holidays when a guest shows appreciation by dropping off gift cards, bottles of wine, edible arrangements, boxes of chocolates, or individual envelopes filled with cash for the staff. Most restaurant workers, especially non-salaried cooks and tipped workers, don't get holiday bonuses, so these gestures can be very impactful.

NO-NO'S

As important as it is to develop good habits when you dine out, it's equally important to limit the bad ones. Not every one of these no-no's—common pitfalls that guests should avoid whenever possible—is going to upset every server in every restaurant, but it always helps to be sensitive to what you're asking for and how you ask for it. Here are a few bad habits that mindful guests should avoid practicing.

Keep Water Specifications to a Minimum

It has always been a pet peeve of mine when guests immediately ask for tap water without ice or specify their water be served at a particular temperature when they first sit down. The issue is not about the ice or the temperature specifications as much as the timing of when these requests are issued. Making demands about water shouldn't be the first interaction you have with your server. Doing so sets an impersonal tone and also increases the likelihood that the server will perceive you as high maintenance. I understand that some people have sensitive teeth or may have recently had dental work done. If that's the case, preface your request by explaining your sensitivity. These are perfectly legitimate reasons, and most servers will understand. But otherwise, it's tap water. It's free. And it's not worth the fuss or potentially injuring your relationship with the server. Instead, take time to chat about the menu, then when you place your order, politely ask the server if they can bring you a glass of water without ice.

Never Wave Cash Around to Get the Bartender's Attention

A bar is not a strip club. Put your money away. Although there are psychological studies that suggest that exposure to monetary cues affects how much effort people will exert in pursuit of material rewards, bartenders generally do not like it when they see someone waving cash around in their face. Doing so is a sign of impatience and privilege. It also sends the message that you think you're more important than everyone else waiting simply because you have money. Start with eye contact. If that doesn't work, try flashing a smile. If smiling doesn't move the needle, a simple raise of the hand should do the trick.

Don't Criticize the Bartender's Pour

In my early days working in restaurants, it was quite common for guests, especially curmudgeonly ones, to make facetious remarks like

"You call that a martini?" whenever they were disappointed by the size of their drink. These days, most bartenders in craft cocktail bars and upscale restaurants use jiggers to measure their pours. There are many reasons why this has become standard practice. Most importantly, using a jigger provides consistency. Measuring pours ensures that drinks are mixed consistently every time. But jiggers also help regulate product usage, the same way that chefs use scales to carefully portion fish fillets or cuts of meat. You may think that your drink is weak, but the bartender doesn't control pour levels; management does. If you feel strongly that a bar's pours are chintzy, the best solution is to drink somewhere else.

Keep the Restaurant-Related Humor to a Minimum

Waiters are routinely subjected to many of the same stale jokes night after night. Not only that, but the guests who deliver them always think they're being novel. When the server clears a plate that's been wiped clean, some jokester will invariably exclaim, "We hated it!" as though the irony will leave the server in stitches. Most staff play along and force a smile, but by the hundredth time, it becomes painful. Here are some other cringeworthy quips waiters hear all the time:

Do you have any low-calorie desserts? Fight the urge to make any desserts-are-fattening jokes and just politely decline the dessert menu. The lowest-calorie dessert is the one you don't order.

You're going to have to roll us out of here! Don't ask if the restaurant has a wheelbarrow, a stretcher, or a gurney—your waiter has heard them all before.

I like my steak still mooing! Cheeky remarks about steak temperatures won't amuse your server. Just order the steak "black and blue" (meaning very rare) and withhold the sophomoric farm animal humor.

That was so good I might have to lick the plate! Like saying "We hated it!" when you didn't, making ironic jokes about finishing your food isn't funny or original.

Don't Order Steaks in between Temperatures

Some diners are fanatical about how they like their steaks cooked. But there is a standard temperature scale for a reason. These rubrics exist so that professional kitchens can cook steaks as consistently and accurately as possible. You should not consider adhering to these standards as optional. Unless you're cooking steaks for yourself at home, there is no such thing as "medium rare *plus*" or "between medium and medium well." A professional cook is too busy to contemplate the existential space between meat temperatures or to be trained on an alternate scale of doneness that exists only in a random guest's imagination, so please stick to the script.

Never Bring Your Own Wine without Asking in Advance

Many restaurants will allow guests to consume a bottle of wine they bring from outside for a "corkage fee," which is usually assessed per bottle. Because a restaurant's profit margins are significantly higher on wine than on food, selling alcohol is essential to its survival. But if a restaurant doesn't have a liquor license, they may allow customers to bring their own alcoholic beverages without charging extra. Some restaurants that do serve alcohol will offer special BYOB (Bring Your Own Bottle) nights to incentivize guests to visit at traditionally slow times like on Sundays and Mondays. If you would like to bring your own bottle (or multiple bottles) of wine, always check with the restaurant in advance about its corkage policy. In doing so, you'll avoid any confusion that may put the staff in an uncompromising position when they have to break the bad news that they don't allow corkage.

Don't Ask Waiters to Bring You Toothpicks

First off, picking your teeth at the table is disgusting. Second, there's a reason that toothpicks are kept in the front of the restaurant near the host stand, so guests can take them on the way out and pick their teeth outside. Your server will likely bring you one if you ask, but making staff run around to chase down toothpicks when they're busy bringing food and drinks to other tables is frivolous. If your dental needs are really that urgent, politely excuse yourself from the table, grab a toothpick from the front, take it to the restroom, and pick away to your heart's content.

Avoid Photographing Staff without Permission

One of the restaurants where I used to work had a dessert cart with various homemade cakes and pies that we'd wheel over to each table to tempt diners into ordering something sweet. One time, after I'd finished my spiel explaining every dessert in vivid detail, a woman trained her cell phone camera on me and asked me to repeat my entire presentation. Since she was so impolite and didn't ask for my permission to take video, I refused. Of course, she was upset, but it wouldn't have been an issue if she'd simply asked my permission first. Had she said, "Would you mind if I snap a quick video of you describing the desserts? I'd like to show my husband back home so I can make him jealous," then it wouldn't have felt so rude or invasive. Instead, she approached it in an entitled way that made me feel like a dancing monkey.

THE TAKEAWAY

If you want to dine like a pro, learn from the pros. Hospitality professionals are a wealth of knowledge about eating, drinking, and dining. We can all benefit from that knowledge. Approaching your dining experiences with the mentality of a restaurant worker will encourage servers to treat you like a peer. Insider secrets like these can help you level up your game.

Postscript

In his farewell essay as restaurant critic for the *New York Times* in July 2024, Pete Wells laments what he sees as the fading humanity in modern restaurants. The digital barriers that impede our ability to find connection and community in our favorite dining spots—whether it's impersonal online reservation systems or QR codes that strip the poetry out of perusing a printed menu—have subsumed the human element of dining out, without which, Wells writes, restaurants struggle to foster intimacy. He grieves for these analog moments—whether it's a superficial conversation with the hostess on the way to the table or a weathered captain's quippy humor and suspiciously enthusiastic endorsement of the daily specials.

In the article, Wells chronicles the myriad ways that restaurants have become more impersonal, but he largely ignores the fact that diners have changed too. He only briefly acknowledges the growing sense of detachment among restaurant patrons and the corrosive effect it can have on the staff. "It's no wonder we are always hearing about diners acting like entitled jerks," he writes. "They've been trained to expect that everybody who works in a restaurant should be as fast and compliant as a touch screen."

Unfortunately, neither Pete nor I have the antidote for restoring the humanity to restaurant experiences. But I can say with certainty that restaurants have never needed more engaged and empathetic clientele than they do right now. Even though traffic in the restaurant industry is up statistically and revenues are reaching record levels, the restaurant economy is broken. Many independent restaurant owners feel buried under the weight of astronomical rents, escalating wages, and sky-rocketing food costs. As inflation rises, so does price consciousness. Consumers expect better value, but few restaurants, aside from multi-national chains, can provide that anymore. As a result, there's a growing disconnect between what restaurants are charging for food and what food *should* cost. Restaurants generally bear the brunt of that shortfall, at their own peril.

We've likely already reached an inflection point. The pandemic had a profound impact on the restaurant industry and dining habits in the United States. Not only did it result in mass closures across the country, but it permanently altered how we consume restaurant food. The American dining public spends more on takeout food and delivered meals than ever. According to the National Restaurant Association, 79 percent of restaurant meals were consumed off premises (meaning not where the meals were prepared) in 2022, which has created stronger headwinds for traditional brick-and-mortar restaurant businesses that rely on dine-in service to justify the expense of costly commercial leases.

Meanwhile, independent restaurants are disappearing at an alarm-ing rate. According to the *Wall Street Journal*, sales growth in fast-food and limited-service restaurants doubled the growth of sit-down restau-rants between 2019 and 2023. At the same time, well-capitalized chain restaurant brands are expanding their reach. Even though 53 percent of restaurants still operate independently, according to the market re-search firm the NPD Group (renamed Circana in 2023), the COVID-19 pandemic disproportionately affected independent restaurants. A study compiled by the financial services company Morgan Stanley found that 10 percent of all independent restaurants shut down in 2020, compared with only 2.5 percent of chain restaurants. If not for the emergency sup-port provided by the federal government's Payment Protection Program (PPP), the devastation would likely have been considerably worse.

There's nothing inherently wrong with chain restaurants. Many of them serve excellent food. But there is something wrong with having a community filled with *only* chain restaurants. It makes neighboring towns unrecognizable from each other. In many cases, the preponder-ance of chain restaurants also erodes America's food culture by denaturing global cuisine from its origins. Long-standing, family-run restaurants that serve international food are supplanted by brands like Chipotle Mexican Grill and Panda Express whose menus bear little resemblance to the culinary traditions that inspired their creation. When large chains dominate the foodscape, the toll is especially hard on immigrant-owned restaurants, and it deprives the dining public of rich global foodways in exchange for bland burrito bowls and cloying plates of orange chicken. When communities lose these legacy restaurants, which have fed generations of families, they forfeit vital parts of their collective history.

But beneath the surface, the eroding health of the restaurant landscape is a direct result of our complacency as consumers. Restaurant lovers have gotten so caught up in celebrity chef culture and the prestige of Michelin stars that they've lost sight of the fact that restaurants are real businesses that rely on turning a profit to survive. Profit margins are already notoriously low in the restaurant industry; for many independent operators, they often fall into single digits, percentagewise. Neighborhood restaurants simply cannot survive without an engaged local customer base. But that loyalty is being tested as menu prices rise, and consumers continue to trade down to more wallet-friendly, fast casual meals.

It's impossible to fully understand how this restaurant monoculture emerged in the United States without examining how American dining habits have evolved over the past century. Our appetite for convenience food accelerated in the post–World War II period with companies like McDonald's and Howard Johnson's capitalizing on the proliferation of auto travel hastened by the rapid expansion of interstate highways. Today that appetite for convenience has become insatiable, with mobile technology providing a more efficient delivery system for restaurant food.

As a result, our relationships with neighborhood restaurants have changed. We expect these restaurants to always be there when we need them, but we rarely show the same commitment in return. In recent decades, our negligence has exacted a heavy toll. Every combo meal we buy from multinational fast-food companies like Chik-fil-A or Bojangles comes at the expense of the family-owned fried chicken place down the road that's struggling to stay afloat. People are crestfallen when a beloved local independent restaurant closes, but the same people often can't remember the last time they dined there. *If independent restaurants must work harder to survive, then we should work harder as consumers to support them.* If we don't, then it's inevitable that one day we'll have no dining options left except for places like Taco Bell and Arby's.

With such a myopic view as diners, we only see how restaurants affect us, not how we affect restaurants. Complaints about "tipping fatigue"—a hot-button issue these days—tend to drown out concerns about whether food service workers are being paid livable wages. While many states have raised the minimum wage for tipped workers in recent years, the federal tipped minimum wage, which allows employers to pay tipped employees subminimum wages, has remained a paltry $2.13 an hour since 1991. Many restaurant patrons remain willfully ignorant about the fact that menu prices are often subsidized by the substandard wages of tipped workers. (A study by the Center for American Progress in 2021 concluded that ending the tipped minimum wage would help alleviate poverty, grow the economy, and advance racial and gender justice.) Nonetheless, many aggrieved patrons prefer to feel victimized by tipping culture instead of advocating for a system that encourages more humane treatment for restaurant workers.

The fact is that almost every time you dine out, you are being served by someone who is struggling to make ends meet, often living paycheck to paycheck. Very few restaurant jobs offer benefits such as paid sick leave, retirement savings, or health insurance (and even if they do, the premiums for those services are usually prohibitively expensive). Professional kitchens are still overwhelmingly staffed by immigrants and undocumented workers, mainly because most of these jobs are considered undesirable to native-born American citizens. For many immigrants with limited employment opportunities, the restaurant industry offers a reliable path toward financial security. But it can also offer a path toward exploitation and abuse by greedy employers. In recent years, a rise in anti-immigration sentiment across the United States has fueled increased hostility toward immigrant workers, which threatens the restaurant industry's most reliable labor source.

Unfortunately, average guests prefer to look the other way rather than confront the plight of the workers who cook and serve their restaurant meals. Most diners don't care about how the sausage is made; they just want to enjoy delicious sausage. For many guests, the pleasure of dining out lies in the luxury of tuning out the evils of the outside world—a seemingly insurmountable task if they're also expected to consider the effects of broken food systems, exploitative labor practices, climate change, human trafficking, misogyny, racism, harassment, and abusive workplaces on their restaurant meals. Sadly, most Americans only care about two things when they visit a restaurant: the quality and the price. They don't have the stomach to grapple with complicated ethical concerns.

But the restaurant industry can only be as healthy as the choices its consumers make. The failure rate among new restaurants is notoriously high. An Ohio State University study in 2005 famously found that 60 percent of restaurants don't make it past the first year, while 80 percent fail within five years. The pandemic has made that calculus even worse. Yet despite the challenging economic climate, the dining public doesn't seem to be taking its responsibility for supporting independent restaurants any more seriously. If anything, as the cost of dining rises, many restaurant patrons expect to pay less and get more.

But there are signs of hope. The internet is a powerful tool for restaurant enthusiasts to immerse themselves in regional foodways and discover new cuisines. It has helped foster a deeper curiosity and appreciation for inspired cooking, culinary exploration, and transformative dining experiences. The restaurants in our communities reflect our rapidly changing culinary traditions, whether in bougie gastropubs in gentrified commercial centers or across bustling urban streets teeming with international food trucks.

I'm hoping this book has convinced you that your behavior as a diner can be instrumental in helping foster a healthier restaurant industry. There are infinite ways you can support restaurants that go far beyond simply spending money in them. You can be more sensitive about how you engage with staff. You can be more agreeable toward restaurants' policies. You can be more charitable about accepting off-peak reservation times. You can act as an ambassador for your favorite restaurants. You can tip generously and not complain about it afterward. You can approach your dining experiences devoid of entitlement—mindful not to take more than you give when you dine out. You can commit yourself to becoming a more compassionate patron who cares deeply about the people who work in restaurants and about the health of your restaurant community. Simply put: you can become a better guest.

Looking back at Emily Post's career, her impact as an arbiter of good taste is undeniable. But her greatest achievement may have been convincing a skeptical public to embrace the idea that there was value in practicing better etiquette. Post's musings were never about putting on airs or climbing the social ladder. She simply provided a pragmatic framework for how to better engage in social situations. Americans may be impressionable, but we're also ruggedly individualistic, and we tend to be stuck in our ways. The widespread acceptance of her book was meaningful at the time, and now, in its nineteenth edition, *Etiquette* remains relevant, sixty-five years after her death.

But I doubt Post would be very impressed with our manners if she was still alive today. While technology facilitates human connection in certain ways, it also hinders our ability to be present in others. Being distracted by our cell phone screens disrupts the most magical element of dining out—the part that makes us feel more connected to other humans and to the world around us. Restaurants are conduits for human connection; they provide sanctuary from the chaos of the outside world. When guests are constantly distracted by the noise, it's much harder for restaurants to provide them respite.

At the world's top dining destinations, staff train for weeks and months on end to learn how to take better care of guests. Shouldn't we, as guests, then also be willing to invest more time and effort into learning how to become better patrons? Sadly, few diners would answer this question affirmatively. Most guests expect restaurants to anticipate their needs even if they aren't invested in better communicating what those needs are. They expect restaurants to blow their minds, yet too often they also expect restaurants to be mind readers.

But I think it's incumbent upon us as diners to be more cognizant of the proper rules of engagement and to recognize that dining out is a veritable skill that can be improved. We should place more trust in the people serving us to lead the way, to honor the tireless effort that goes into creating special restaurant experiences by deferring to their expertise whenever possible. We should always remember that when we choose our language more carefully or when we ask for things the right way, we increase the chances of getting what we want without creating unnecessary friction. We must learn to embrace the idea that our behavior influences the success or failure of our dining experiences. From my decades of experience serving all kinds of guests, I believe that there's a science to proper engagement in a restaurant and that once you've mastered the basics, like the ones I've outlined in this book, it becomes an art.

So now that you have all this valuable knowledge about how to be a better restaurant guest, *what can you do with all of it?*

As consumers, we hold the key to a brighter future for the restaurant industry. If the pandemic taught us anything, it's that we should never assume that restaurants are immune to existential risk. The biggest threat to their sanctity may be technology. As restaurants become more popular, tech entrepreneurs look to find ways to leverage technology to improve efficiency with digital solutions such as robotic kitchen equipment, QR code menus, and contactless mobile payments. Others are actively pursuing unicorn projects with younger innovations such as artificial intelligence, virtual reality, and NFTs (non-fungible tokens). So far, most of those endeavors have fallen flat. But early failures likely won't stop restaurateurs from trying to invent new ways to integrate technology into our dining experiences.

Without healthier consumer habits, though, the future looks bleak. The risks of investing in food service businesses are higher than ever, which centralizes power and influence among a shrinking cabal of well-capitalized restaurant groups. Rather than innovating, many mid-tier restaurant companies are now focused on franchising preexisting concepts that have proven successful in their home cities and transporting them to major markets across the country. Today you'll find facsimiles of many name-brand New York City restaurants such as Carbone and COTE Korean Steakhouse in places like Miami, Las Vegas, Dallas, and even Dubai. Over time, this trend has a flattening-out effect on the country's dining landscape, hastening a sameness that threatens the preservation and potency of our regional foodways. The trend will undoubtedly worsen as costs become more prohibitive and small businesses continue to be pushed out by large corporate interests.

Every time you dine in an independent restaurant, you are participating in the realization of someone's dream. The menu is often a reflection of a chef's personal story, an amalgam of recipes that pay homage to their family history or to culinary traditions that have been passed down over generations. Dining out with the attitude that a restaurant has to prove its worth dishonors not only the fortitude that it takes to turn those dreams into reality but also the generosity of spirit required to allow you, as a guest, to share in the realization of that dream.

Being a restaurant guest is *a privilege*. When we approach our dining experiences more mindfully, we become more deeply invested in a restaurant's success and perhaps more forgiving of its missteps. No restaurant can be perfect every time, and one disappointing experience does not mean that a restaurant is bad. Enlightened guests understand that even the best restaurants in the world—no matter how many Michelin stars or James Beard Awards they have on their mantel—can be underwhelming occasionally. I promise you: even Noma in Copenhagen, often considered the best restaurant in the world, has off nights.

So, whether we spend twenty dollars on a meal or two hundred, we can train ourselves to be more empathetic guests and to find silver linings in those unfortunate moments when restaurants under-deliver. Together we can help the industry thrive by adopting a new mindset about our patronage, built upon the idea that we, as restaurant guests, should consider ourselves partners, not simply patrons. I believe there is always room for improvement.

ACKNOWLEDGMENTS

This book is dedicated to my uncle Robert Leopold Barnett, my closest friend, who passed away from cancer in 2015, at age fifty-seven. We nicknamed him L.G., short for "legal guardian," as he was a surrogate parent to me and my sisters throughout most of my adult life. When I moved to New York City after college in 1996, Robert and I regularly traversed the city to discover new restaurants. We brunched at charming French bistros in the West Village, ate pillowy gnocchi at hole-in-the-wall trattorias, and canvassed the city for speakeasy bars before speakeasies were cool. Without him, I never would have developed my affinity for restaurants and the passion I have for the art of dining. I'm also grateful for the unwavering encouragement of my two sisters, Alana and Loren, and the love and support of my brother-in-law Mike, aunt Terri, and cousin Diana. One of the greatest gifts of my life has been becoming an uncle myself, to three bright and beautiful nieces: Landri, Aila, and Leena.

I'd like to express my sincerest gratitude to Jenny Keegan, my editor at Louisiana State University Press, for seeing the value in this book. It's not lost on me that publishing a volume about restaurant etiquette is an unusual undertaking for an academic press, but Jenny was an early proponent of my work and advocated for this project at a time when my credentials as a writer were scant. Thanks also to Elizabeth Gratch for her graceful copyedits. A special shout-out to the many patient editors who have supported my work through the years and helped me cultivate my skills as a writer and reporter—among others: Matt Rodbard of *Taste*, Kate Krader of *Bloomberg*, Lesley Suter of *Eater*, Alan Sytsma of *New York Magazine*, Chloe Frechette of *Punch*, and Tim McKirdy of *VinePair*.

Finally, I'd like to acknowledge all the beautiful, resilient, and colorful people who make magic in restaurants every day. Throughout my twenty-year career in hospitality, I was fortunate to work with so many extraordinary people—parents, PhD candidates, law students, computer programmers, dancers, artists, actors, musicians, photographers, aspiring restaurateurs, and more—who, like me, found a sense of belonging in the restaurant industry. I've worked with people whose restaurant work is their livelihood and some whose restaurant work is their *life*. But no matter which camp they belong to, they all perform their job with immense pride and always give more than they take. The sacrifices that restaurant workers make every day to provide hospitality to strangers—sometimes at the expense of their own dignity—are a gift. All too often, their generosity isn't reciprocated. So, when your server recites the specials, put your phone away and pay attention. Look them in the eye. Say please and thank you. And always, ALWAYS, *always*, tip generously.

GLOSSARY OF
RESTAURANT TERMS

back of the house (BOH). The area of the restaurant where food is prepared, cooked, and cleaned. The term can also refer to the team of chefs, line cooks, dishwashers, porters, and other employees whose duties are confined to the kitchen.

brigade system. Inspired by factory assembly lines and popularized by chef Auguste Escoffier, it denotes the hierarchal structure within a professional kitchen in which individual tasks, like grilling meats or preparing salads, are highly specified to increase efficiency.

camping. A common term inside the restaurant industry that describes parties who linger at their table long past their allotted time.

captain. A fancy word for server or headwaiter that is used in many old-school fine dining establishments, especially more traditional French or French-influenced restaurants.

chef de cuisine. A French term meaning "chief of the kitchen." The chef de cuisine is responsible for the day-to-day management of the kitchen, including overseeing culinary operations, creating menus, and managing staff.

comp. Restaurant vernacular that usually refers to a food or beverage item that is served complimentary, or free of charge, either because a guest didn't like it or because it was offered gratis as an apology or a gift.

corkage fee. When restaurants allow guests to bring their own wine to consume during their meal, they typically charge a nominal fee per bottle called "corkage." The fee varies by restaurant and is usually meant to offset lost revenue from forgone wine sales.

corked wine. The term refers to a flaw that can found in a small percentage of wine bottles. Corked wine results from the presence of 2,4,6-trichloranisole (TCA), a contaminant found in tainted cork that produces off-odors redolent of wet cardboard or moldy basement.

credit card roulette. A game of chance that some restaurant guests play in which everyone puts their credit card in a pile, then a third party randomly draws one of the cards to pay the entire bill.

deuce. Standard industry lingo for a table that seats two people. Higher guest counts are typically referred to with the suffix *-top*. For example, a party of four will be called a four-top and a party of six a six-top.

eighty-six. Restaurant industry slang meaning an item has sold out. The term's origin has been debated, from a soda jerk's numeric code in the 1930s meaning "all out of it" to a speakeasy's covert instructions to evacuate customers by "eighty-sixing" them through the back door of 86 Bedford Street in New York City. It can also refer to a customer being ejected from the bar or restaurant.

expediter, or expo. One of the most important BOH positions, the expo communicates with line cooks to orchestrate the firing of tables, ensuring that orders are passed seamlessly and efficiently between the kitchen and waitstaff.

farm-to-table. A ubiquitous moniker in fine dining that denotes a restaurant's or chef's effort to exclusively source local produce for their menu, often purchasing ingredients directly from the farmers.

fast casual. This category of restaurants refers to a segment of the industry that offers quick-service meals a level above most common fast-food restaurants like McDonald's, often featuring more customizable menus with higher-quality ingredients.

fire. The command a chef or expediter gives to instruct their line cooks to begin preparing a table's food. When a ticket is "fired," it means the server will have ample time to clear and reset the table before the next course arrives.

foodie. A slang term, sometimes used pejoratively, to describe avid diners and culinary enthusiasts. The term first appeared in print in a 1980 review of *Restaurant d'Olympe* by Gael Greene in *New York Magazine*.

front of the house (FOH). The part of a restaurant that customers interact with. It may also refer to the team of forward-facing staff such as waiters, bartenders, hosts, bussers, and food runners who work in the dining room.

getting stiffed. When a table leaves zero tip or severely undertips, servers will often refer to this as "stiffing" or "getting stiffed."

gratuity. A voluntary payment given to someone for a service they provided. In the United States, a typical gratuity in a restaurant ranges between 15 and 25 percent. For larger parties, gratuity is often automatically included on the bill. (Restaurant workers refer to this as an "auto-grat.")

greasy spoon. A colloquial term for a no-frills diner or inexpensive restaurant with short-order fare. It was popularized in the 1920s as a derogatory way to connote a dirty restaurant but may also be used as a term of endearment.

jigger. A bar tool used to measure alcohol and other liquids for cocktails to ensure consistency.

joiner. Industry parlance for a late-arriving customer who, often unexpectedly, joins an existing party that has already been seated.

Le Cordon Bleu. A renowned French hospitality and culinary arts school founded in Paris by Marthe Distel in 1895 that now has thirty-five institutes in twenty different countries.

maître d.' The abbreviation for *maître d'hôtel*, a French term meaning "master of the house." The maître d' acts as the gatekeeper in most fine dining restaurants, primarily responsible for managing the reservation book and greeting guests when they arrive.

menu spiel. A slang term commonly used to describe a server's tableside explanation or description of the menu, often including the nightly specials and strategies for ordering. The etymology of the phrase comes from the German *spiel*, which means "game," and the Yiddish *shpil*, meaning "play."

mise en place. A French culinary term that, loosely translated, means "everything in its place." It refers to a regimented system of organizing prepared ingredients in a professional kitchen to maximize the cooks' efficiency.

molecular gastronomy. A scientific approach to cooking that uses experimental techniques, popularized by chef Ferran Adrià in Spain in the 1990s, incorporating chemistry and physics to push the limits of cooking beyond traditional methods. The phrase was coined in 1988 by the Hungarian physicist Nicholas Kurti and French chemist Hervé This.

omakase. A Japanese word meaning "I leave it up to you." It typically refers to a Japanese dining experience in which the chef selects the menu. Common in sushi restaurants, omakase often refers to a curated plate of raw fish or a series of individual sushi pieces hand delivered by the chef.

order fire. Kitchen parlance for a single-course order. When a table only orders one course, the kitchen needs to fire the ticket right away. Too many order fire tickets at once can wreak havoc because it often puts undue pressure on one part of the kitchen, such as the grill or pasta station.

palm tips. A tip given to someone by discreetly placing a small amount of cash in the palm of one's hand during a handshake. Servers call this gesture "palming."

the pass. The area of the kitchen where dishes are plated and given a final inspection before being sent out to the table. The pass is usually overseen by the chef or an expediter who organizes the tickets with each table's order and orchestrates the orderly firing of food.

pooling tips. A practice in most fine dining restaurants in which FOH employees combine their tips and then divide them among the staff according to a prescribed formula.

POS system. A POS, or "point-of-sale," system is a combination of hardware and software that restaurants use to place orders and process transactions. The technology has shifted to mobile in recent years, with handheld devices that allow for remote ordering and contactless digital payments.

power lunch. A moniker used to describe high-powered business meetings conducted over lunch. The term was coined by Lee Eisenberg in a 1979 *Esquire* article to refer to the commerce-fueled lunch scene at the Four Seasons Restaurant in Midtown Manhattan.

prix fixe menu. French term meaning "fixed price." A prix fixe menu typically offers a complete meal for a set price, often with choices from a small list of appetizers, entrées, and desserts.

refire. When food is returned to the kitchen and needs to be prepared again, it is referred to as a "refire." Waiters are often expected to provide the chef with a handwritten refire ticket that details how to repair the issue.

signature dish. A dish that a chef is known for or that is unique to a restaurant. The concept of signature dishes took off with the rise of celebrity chefs in the 1990s; specific recipes became a chef's calling card or the reason for visiting their flagship restaurant.

sommelier. The French word for "wine steward." Most sommeliers have achieved some degree of training or accreditation, although many "somms" learn on the job. Aside from assisting customers with wine choices and creating beverage pairings, they also manage inventory and maintain the wine cellar.

spiking a ticket. Once every dish from a table's order has been sent out from the kitchen, the chef or expediter will "spike" the ticket on an upright metal prong that rests somewhere near the pass.

sous-chef. The chef de cuisine's second-in-command. Sous-chefs assist with all aspects of staff management and training and are typically tasked with running the kitchen on nights when the head chef is absent. The term comes from the French word *sous*, meaning "under."

turning tables. An industry term for the process of resetting a table after a group of diners has left and seating a new group. The term *turn-and-burn* refers to the practice of turning tables more aggressively, a tactic employed more often in fast-paced, casual restaurants than in upscale ones.

verbal tip. Servers use this term pejoratively to describe situations when guests express praise or positive feedback verbally without following through with an adequate tip.

walk-in. A refrigerated storage area in a restaurant's prep kitchen where perishable items are kept that allows staff to walk inside to access and store large quantities of food.

SELECTED BIBLIOGRAPHY

BOOKS

Bourdain, Anthony. *Kitchen Confidential: Adventures in the Culinary Underbelly.* New York: HarperCollins, 2000.

Freedman, Paul. *Ten Restaurants That Changed America.* Introduction by Danny Meyer. New York: Liveright, 2016.

The Glass Floor: Sexual Harassment in the Restaurant Industry. Report. Prepared by Restaurant Opportunities Center United and Forward Together, October 7, 2014.

Guidara, Will. *Unreasonable Hospitality: The Remarkable Power of Giving People More Than They Expect.* New York: Optimism Press, 2022.

Meyer, Danny. *Setting the Table: The Transforming Power of Hospitality in Business.* New York: HarperCollins, 2006.

Post, Emily. *Etiquette: In Society, in Business, in Politics, and at Home.* New York: Funk & Wagnalls, 1922.

Post, Lizzie, and Daniel Post Senning. *Emily Post's Etiquette: The Centennial Edition.* Emeryville, CA: Ten Speed Press, 2022.

Rawson, Katie, and Elliot Shore. *Dining Out: A Global History of Restaurants.* London: Reaktion, 2019.

Ribbat, Christoph. *In the Restaurant: Society in Four Courses.* Translated by Jamie Searle Romanelli. London: Pushkin Press, 2016.

Scott, William R. *The Itching Palm: A Study of the Habit of Tipping in America.* Philadelphia: Penn Publishing Co., 1916.

Sitwell, William. *The Restaurant: A 2,000-Year History of Dining Out.* New York: Diversion, 2020.

Spang, Rebecca L. *The Invention of the Restaurant: Paris and Modern Gastronomic Culture.* Cambridge: Harvard University Press, 2000.

Desilver, Drew, and Jordan Lippert. *How Americans See Recent Developments in Tipping*. Report. Pew Research Center, November 9, 2023.

Eser, Alexander. "Americans Eat Out Statistics: An $800 Billion Industry Breakdown." Worldmetrics.com, July 23, 2024.

Haddon, Heather, and Ruth Simon. "The Skyrocketing Costs Driving Cheeseburger Prices Up." *Wall Street Journal*, March 4, 2024.

Jakab, Spencer. "Why Your Favorite Restaurant Might Close." *Wall Street Journal*, January 13, 2023.

Kelton, Katie. "Survey: More than 1 in 3 Americans Think Tipping Culture Has Gotten Out of Control." Bankrate.com, June 5, 2024.

Li, Jin, Lei Liu, Yu Sun, Wei Fan, Mei Li, and Yiping Zhong. "Exposure to Money Modulates Neural Responses to Outcome Evaluations Involving Social Reward." *Social Cognitive and Affective Neuroscience* 15, no. 1, February 12, 2020, 111–21. https://pmc.ncbi.nlm.nih.gov/articles/PMC7171377/#ref64.

Lynn, Michael, Michael C. Sturman, Christie Ganley, Elizabeth Adams, Mathew Douglas, and Jessica McNeal. "Consumer Racial Discrimination in Tipping: A Replication and Extension." *Journal of Applied Social Psychology* 38, no. 4, March 19, 2008, 1045–60. Available at Cornell University, eCommons, January 1, 2008.

"100,000 Restaurants Closed Six Months into Pandemic." Press release. National Restaurant Association, September 14, 2020.

Renton, Alex. "How Sushi Ate the World." *The Guardian*, February 26, 2006.

Repanich, Jeremy. "The Intricate Art (and Hidden History) of Kaiseki." *Robb Report*, March 22, 2018.

Saxena, Jaya. "Please Put Your Light Away at the Restaurant." *Eater*, September 18, 2024.

Schweitzer, Justin. *Ending the Tipped Minimum Wage Will Reduce Poverty and Inequality*. Report. Center for American Progress, March 30, 2021.

State of the Restaurant Industry 2025. Report. National Restaurant Association, February 5, 2025.

Torgan, Carol. "Humans Can Identify More than 1 Trillion Smells." NIH Health Matters. National Institutes of Health, March 31, 2014.

Wells, Pete. "I Reviewed Restaurants for 12 Years. They've Changed, and Not for the Better." *New York Times*, August 6, 2024.